PASTA COOKERY

by Sophie Kay

ANOTHER BEST-SELLING COOKERY VOLUME FROM H.P. BOOKS

Author: Sophie Kay Petros; Publisher: Helen Fisher; Editors: Carroll Latham,
Carlene Tejada; Art Director: Don Burton; Book Design: Kathy Olson; Typography:
Cindy Coatsworth, Joanne Porter; Food Stylist: Mable Hoffman; Photography:
George deGennaro Studios.

Published by H.P. Books, P.O. Box 5367, Tucson, AZ 85703   602/888-2150
ISBN: 0-89586-030-9
Library of Congress Catalog Card Number, 79-67183 ©1979 Fisher Publishing, Inc.
Printed in U.S.A.

Pasta—A World Traveler

Flour and a liquid mixed together, cooked, and served as part of a meal, is pasta. Other ingredients such as eggs and flavorings may be added to the basic flour and liquid mixture—the result is still pasta. Both noodles and macaroni products are pasta. The word *pasta* has been used to refer to a variety of doughs generally made from a hard wheat flour called *semolina.* These doughs were made into various shapes and sizes. Examples would be spaghetti, macaroni and linguine. Now *pasta* is a more general term and refers to a cooked dough made with any flour and water.

Macaroni, one of the most popular pasta types, is shaped like a tube—hollow through the middle—and is available in various sizes and thicknesses. Pasta dough for making macaroni does not usually contain eggs. Macaroni products almost double in size during cooking. Examples are elbow macaroni, mostaccioli and shells.

Noodles are made from a dough consisting of flour, water and eggs or egg yolks. The dough is cut into flat ribbons of various widths from very fine up to extra-wide. Noodles do not expand appreciably during cooking. When you buy noodles, the package is usually labeled *egg noodles.*

The origin of pasta is varied, depending upon where you get your information. Macaroni is mentioned in a Chinese cookbook as far back as 3000 B.C. Marco Polo is supposed to have dis-covered it on one of his visits and brought it back to Venice in 1295. According to the records of the Spaghetti Museum in Pontedassio, Italy, ravioli was eaten in Italy almost 20 years before Marco Polo's famous travels. One account says that people in Southern Italy learned to make pasta from the Arabs who were their neighbors across the Mediterranean Sea. The Arabs made pasta to preserve flour during their long treks across the desert.

Today, many households in Europe make their own pasta. The Greeks make small pasta squares, the Germans enjoy *spaetzle,* and Polish cooks make *pierogi.* In Southern Italy, thin strands like spaghetti and vermicelli are popular. The Northern Italians prefer wider strands of pasta and this is the kind of pasta most common in Northern European countries. In China and other Far Eastern countries, pasta is most often served in the form of won ton skins and egg roll wrappers. Wherever you go, you'll find people eating pasta.

In this cookbook, you'll find my version of pastas made in different countries. You'll also discover both original and adapted recipes to show you how to use your homemade pasta.

No time to make your own pasta? Your local supermarket has row upon row of the various pasta shapes and sizes to enhance your menus and stretch your budget. Why not try pasta for dinner tonight?

Nutritive Value

Your daily foods should include those from the basic 4 groups: meats, fruits and vegetables, dairy products and breads and cereals. Pasta falls in the bread and cereal category and you should have 4 or more servings from this group every day. A serving of pasta daily helps fulfill this requirement.

Pasta provides a good distribution of essential amino acids to help provide protein, B vitamins (thiamine, riboflavin, and niacin) and iron. Pasta is low in fat and sodium and is easily digested. The carbohydrates in pasta rank high in providing energy. Most commercial pastas are enriched with fortified vitamins.

A 1/2-cup serving of cooked macaroni or spaghetti contains 70 to 80 calories. A 1/2-cup serving of cooked egg noodles contains about 80 calories.

If you're watching calories, some diet programs have what is called a pasta exchange in which you can substitute one 1/2-cup serving of cooked pasta for one slice of bread up to three times a week.

Sophie Kay

Sophie Kay's activities and travels keep her in touch with today's cooks. With her tours, TV programs, books and cooking classes, she is in constant communication with people who are interested in food. Her audiences warm quickly to her generous personality and seek her advice on such problems as cooking creatively, shopping on a limited budget and using leftovers.

As much at ease at her desk as she is in her kitchen and before the TV cameras, Sophie Kay decided to write a cookbook that would solve the good-food-on-a-budget problem. *Pasta Cookery* is Sophie's second book with HPBooks. In *Yogurt Cookery,* she shared her secrets for making and using yogurt. Her other cookbooks include: *Sophie Kay's Step By Step Cookbook, Sophie Kay's Family Cookbook, Menus From Around The World,* and *The Ideals Junior Chef Cookbook.*

If you're in the Milwaukee area, you can see Sophie on her own TV show and various food and appliance commercials. She is listed in Who's Who Of American Women and has a degree in home economics and journalism from Northwestern University.

Pasta Comes In Many Shapes

These photos and the accompanying text will help you determine which pasta shape you can substitute for another and which pasta shape would work best in an improvised dish. These are not all the available pastas. The list is practically endless. When you discover a different pasta shape, experiment with it. You may create your own special recipe.

Soup pastas are cut very small so they will be convenient and attractive in soups.

1. **Orzo,** sometimes called **barley pasta,** actually resembles rice and can be used as a rice substitute in many dishes.
2. **Bows** or **butterflies** come in a variety of sizes. The smaller ones are best suited for soups.
3. **Tiny shells** add an interesting look to canned or homemade soup. They are available in most supermarkets.
4. **Ditalini** is small macaroni cut very short.
5. **Egg noodle flakes** begin as very fine pasta sheets. The sheets are cut into 1/4-inch squares.
6. **Alphabets,** little noodles cut in the shape of letters, appeal to children.
7. **Tubettini,** or tiny macaroni, is much smaller than ditalini, above.

These pastas are ideal for stuffing with meat, cheese and vegetable mixtures.

1. **Green manicotti tubes** are generally made with spinach to add flavor and color. These large tubes are about 4 inches long and 1 inch wide.
2. **Plain manicotti tubes** are the same size as the green tubes. Both types of manicotti have ends that are cut diagonally.
3. **Egg roll wrappers** can be cut into 5- or 6-inch squares, then wrapped around or folded over a filling.
4. **Jumbo or giant shells** resemble a conch shell. Some are plain; others have deep grooves.
5. **Ravioli,** small pasta squares, usually have pinked or notched edges. They are stuffed with meat, cheese or vegetables and served with a sauce. They can also be fried.
6. **Won ton skins** are small squares that are Chinese in origin. They can be filled and formed into various shapes. Won ton are popular in soups, but they can also be fried.
7. **Cappelletti** means *small hats.* These shaped dumplings are usually filled with minced chicken or meat.

Main-dish pastas can be combined with meats, vegetables and cheese to make a satisfying meal.

1. **Green Lasagne**, broad, flat noodles about 1-1/2 inches wide, is made with spinach.
2. **Spaghetti** is long, thin, solid strands of pasta. The strands come in various widths.
3. **Mostaccioli**, large macaroni about 2 inches long, may have a ridged or plain surface. The ends are always cut diagonally.
4. **Lasagne with ruffled edges**, a flat, broad pasta, is 1-1/2 to 2 inches wide. The ruffled edges serve only to dress up the noodle.
5. **Medium egg noodles** are flat, thin rectangles about 2" x 1/2".
6. **Green fettuccini** is ribbons of spinach pasta about 1/4 inch wide.
7. **Wide coiled noodles**, made from egg noodle pasta, are cut about 3/8 inch wide before they are twisted into coils.
8. **Vermicelli clusters**, very delicate in appearance, are strands of fine spaghetti twisted into a cluster.
9. **Fine egg noodles** are the extra-fine cut of egg noodle pasta.
10. **Rigatoni** is a grooved macaroni that is similar to plain manicotti tubes but smaller. The tubes may be slightly curved.

The following pasta shapes are popular in casserole dishes.

1. **Rotini spirals** are about 1-1/2 inches long. They add visual interest to casseroles and one-dish meals.
2. **Ziti**, also called **thick macaroni**, comes in long tubes.
3. **Green egg noodles** get their color from spinach. They are a colorful addition to casseroles and soups.
4. **Linguine** is narrow flat strands of pasta. It is sometimes referred to as **flat spaghetti**.
5. **Fusilli**, long strands of spiraled spaghetti, is easy to handle so it is often called **non-skid spaghetti**.
6. **Bows** or **butterflies** are about 1-1/2 inches long with fluted edges. They come in a variety of sizes.
7. **Thin spaghetti**, or **spaghettini**, is long fine-cut pasta strands.
8. **Wheels** are die-cut shapes that resemble a wheel with spokes and a grooved rim.

How To Cook Pasta

Decide if pasta is to be the main dish or a side dish. If, like the Italians, you serve pasta as an introductory course before the main meat course, the pasta portions will be small. Macaroni and spaghetti are almost doubled in bulk after they are cooked. Egg noodles remain about the same. In general, 8 ounces of uncooked spaghetti, elbow macaroni (2 cups) or egg noodles (4 cups) will serve about 4 people as a main-dish serving. A pound of uncooked spaghetti can serve as few as 4 or as many as 8, depending on how hearty the sauce and how robust the appetites.

The most essential piece of equipment needed for cooking pasta is a pot that is large enough so the pasta can cook freely in boiling water. If you often have problems cooking pasta, change to a larger pot. A too-small pot is the most common cause of improperly cooked pasta. There are pots of various sizes available with perforated inserts and a cover. After the pasta is cooked, the insert is lifted from the pot and set aside to drain.

Use a wooden fork to stir pasta; a metal fork may break or pierce the delicate pasta, and pushing it with a spoon may cause it to lump together. Several types of spaghetti lifters or rakes are available for removing pasta from the pot. A variety of plastic and metal tongs for tossing and serving spaghetti or noodles are available in department stores, supermarkets and cookware shops.

Many people overcook pasta or don't use enough water. If pasta cooks freely in boiling water, it will not stick together or taste starchy.

The proportions of water to pasta I use are:

8 ounces of pasta
6 cups or more boiling water
1 teaspoon salt
1 tablespoon vegetable oil

Spaghetti and long homemade noodles require twice as much water.

First, bring the water to a rapid boil in a large heavy pot. Add the salt and oil. Add salt after the water comes to a boil because if the salt boils in the water too long, it gives the pasta an off-taste or a disagreeable odor. Vegetable oil in the water prevents the pasta from sticking together and keeps the water from boiling over. Gradually add the spaghetti or macaroni, being sure the water continues to boil. Rapid and continuously boiling water keeps the pasta moving so it cooks evenly and quickly.

To add long pasta to a pot, place the ends of a bunch in the water, resting the other ends against the rim of the pot. When the ends in the water begin to soften, coil the pasta into the pot, pushing the softening strands into the water with a wooden fork.

Cook pasta uncovered, gently stirring it occasionally with a wooden fork to separate the pasta pieces or strands. Cover the pot only to bring the water to a more rapid boil. If a lid is used while the pasta is cooking, the water will probably boil over.

Another method for cooking spaghetti, noodles

Adding spaghetti to boiling water.

or macaroni is to add them to boiling salted water and bring the water to a vigorous boil again. Cook and stir constantly for 5 minutes. Remove the pot from the heat, cover it and let it stand about 8 minutes, stirring once.

IS IT DONE?

Cooking time varies with the size and thickness of the pasta. Some small soup macaronies may take only a few minutes to cook, while larger shapes such as lasagne may take up to 15 minutes. Homemade pasta always cooks faster than the pasta you buy. Cooking time for dried homemade pasta, depending on how thick you have rolled the dough, may be as short as 3 minutes. Homemade pasta that has not been dried may cook in seconds. Start testing it after 30 seconds of cooking.

Cooked pasta should be pliable but firm when you press one piece against the side of the pot with a fork. If you taste a piece of pasta before you remove it from the pot, you can tell when it's tender and yet firm or *al dente*. No white center should remain when a strand is cut nor should it have any flour taste.

Some cooks say that another way to test cooked pasta is to throw a few strands at a tile wall. If the pasta sticks to the wall, it's done—I have never had the courage to try this!

If pasta is to be used in a casserole, cook it a shorter time than you would if you were serving it right from the pot. It will continue to cook in the hot sauce of the casserole.

DRAINING PASTA

After pasta is cooked it may be lifted directly from the pot. Shake the pasta gently as you lift it to remove excess water. Place the cooked pasta on a warm plate.

I drain cooked pasta immediately in a large colander. Shake the colander and do not rinse the pasta.

Once pasta is drained it should be served immediately with butter and grated cheese or tossed with a piping hot sauce.

If you plan to use pasta in a cold salad, rinse the pasta in cold water and drain it again in the colander. To prevent pasta from sticking together while it chills in the refrigerator, stir some of the salad dressing into the pasta before refrigerating it.

KEEPING IT WARM

If you cannot serve cooked pasta immediately, preheat your oven to 175°F (80°C), drain the pasta and return it to the empty cooking pot. Stir in soft butter, cover the pot and keep the pasta warm in the preheated oven for not more than 30 minutes.

You can reheat plain cold pasta in a double boiler with a little hot water, meat stock or vegetable stock, milk or butter.

HOW TO TOSS PASTA WITH THE SAUCE

Pasta may be served with the sauce poured over each serving or all the pasta may be tossed with the sauce before serving.

It is easier to coat the pasta evenly with the sauce if you return the drained pasta to the pot it was cooked in. Pour the sauce over the drained pasta in the pot, then toss it gently with a large wooden fork and spoon. Use the fork and spoon to raise and roll the pasta over the sauce until all the pasta is coated. Immediately pour the pasta and sauce into a hot deep serving bowl.

Now that your appetite is whetted and your cooking urge is inspired, you are probably too impatient to browse further. To start you off, How To Make Pasta, begins on page 9 and Sauces are on pages 134 to 144.

Lifting spaghetti from the pot.

Guide To Pasta Equipment

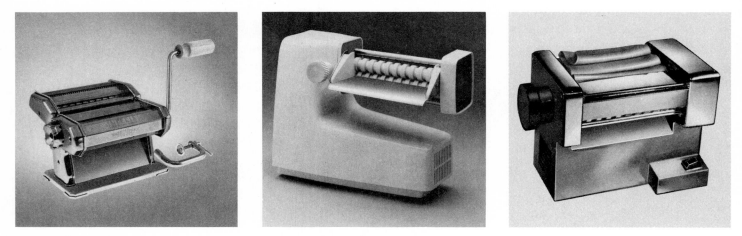

Pasta machines, or *pasta makers* are also called *noodle makers.* They fall into 2 basic categories: manually operated and electric. They are usually made of chrome-plated metal and are self sharpening and self lubricating.

Pasta machines do not mix pasta dough. After the dough is mixed, it is kneaded, rolled and cut in the pasta machine. With the adjusting dial, you can change the width between the rollers according to the desired thickness of the pasta. Most machines are equipped with 2 cutters. Many manufacturers offer additional cutters.

The manually operated machine pictured on the left has to be clamped to your table or work surface. Clamps come packaged with the machine.

The electric machines in the center and on the right operate faster than the manually operated machine. The electric machine pictured in the center has nylon rollers and cutters. The finished product has a slightly pebbled texture. Whichever pasta machine you choose, read the manufacturer's instructions carefully.

Never wash pasta machines. Water causes sticking and rusting. To clean your machine, dust it with flour and use a small brush to remove pieces of dough.

There are also smaller manually operated plastic pasta machines, not pictured.

Pasta Accessories

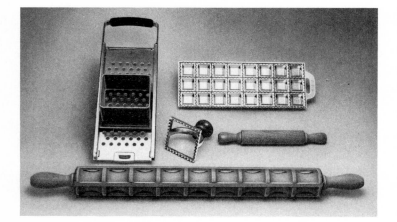

Several types of *spaetzle makers* are available to make tiny irregularly shaped dumplings. The spaetzle maker at top left fits on the rim of a pot. The hopper is filled with dough and slides over the perforated blade, cutting off the spaetzle.

Ravioli makers or forms are usually metal frames with squares that vary in size from 1 to 2-3/4 inches. The squares mold a sheet of dough into a series of depressions which hold the filling. Some frames have 2 sections: one holds the dough and another presses the dough into the bottom frame. After the dough is filled and covered with a second pasta sheet, the ravioli is sealed and cut by rolling a rolling pin over the frame. The frame pictured has only 1 section and makes miniature ravioli.

A wooden *ravioli cutting pin* shown at the bottom has rows of squares. It is rolled over the filled dough, cutting and sealing as it rolls.

The *ravioli stamp,* in the center, seals and cuts the filled ravioli 1 at a time.

How To Make Pasta

The instructions on these pages are meant to be used as a guide, depending on the equipment you have and the recipe you use. The recipes for the different varieties of pasta begin on page 14.

If you don't have time to complete the pasta-making process the day you begin it, place the mixed and kneaded pasta dough in a plastic bag and refrigerate it overnight. The next morning, remove the dough from the refrigerator and let it stand at room temperature about 1 hour before rolling.

Pasta dough may also be frozen. The night before you plan to roll and cut the dough, remove it from the freezer and let it thaw in the refrigerator until morning. Then bring the dough to room temperature before you roll it.

By Hand

Making a well in the flour.

MIXING

Place the flour on a large clean board or countertop. Make a well in the center of the flour. Break eggs into the well; add oil or salt. Beat the eggs with a fork. Gently work some flour from the side of the well into the beaten eggs. Continue until most of the flour is used and the dough is sticky. It will be difficult to continue mixing the dough with the fork.

Beating eggs in the well.

Working in the flour.

The mixed dough before kneading.

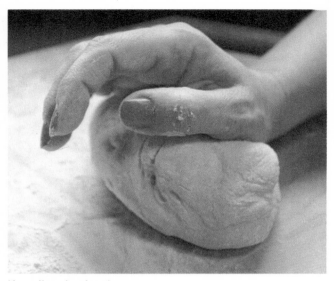
Kneading the dough.

KNEADING

Place the dough on a lightly floured surface. With the heel of your hand, gently but firmly push the dough away from you. Give it a 1/4 turn. Grasp the portion of the dough farthest away from you and fold it toward you. Continue pushing, turning and folding until the dough is rough-looking. Cover the dough with plastic wrap and let it rest 10 minutes. Knead the dough again until most of the flour is used and the dough is smooth and elastic, about 10 minutes. Divide the dough into 3 or 4 balls and place them in a plastic bag to prevent them from drying out. Let the balls rest in the plastic bag about 30 minutes.

The resting dough covered with plastic wrap.

ROLLING

Place 1 ball of dough on a lightly floured surface and flatten it slightly by hand. To roll out dough, use a long, thin, floured rolling pin, a well-sanded dowel or broom handle or any smooth cylindrical shape that has a diameter of at least 1-1/2 inches. The longer the rolling pin or cylinder, the easier it will be to stretch the dough as you roll it. Roll out dough from the center to the outer edge, stretching it with your hands as you roll. Flip the dough over often for even rolling and dust it with flour to prevent sticking. Roll out the dough to about 1/16 inch thick or desired thickness, depending on the type of pasta you are making. Lightly sprinkle it with flour and let it rest 15 minutes on a lightly floured dry towel. Repeat with the remaining balls of dough.

Rolling out the dough.

Cutting flat dough.

Cutting rolled-up dough.

CUTTING

With a sharp knife, cut the dough into 1/8- to 1/4-inch strips or roll it loosely into a flat jelly-roll shape and cut the roll into desired widths. Spread or unwind each strip on a dry cloth towel. Let the strips stand uncovered 15 to 30 minutes before cooking or 3 to 4 hours to dry completely before storing.

With A Pasta Maker

MIXING

Mix the dough by hand, page 9

KNEADING

Place the dough on a lightly floured surface. With the heel of your hand, gently but firmly push the dough away from you. Give it a 1/4 turn. Grasp the portion of the dough farthest away from you and fold it toward you. Continue pushing, turning and folding until the dough is rough-looking. Cover with plastic wrap and let it rest 10 minutes or start to roll immediately. Divide the dough into 3 or 4 balls. Place all but 1 ball in a plastic bag to prevent them from drying out. Slightly flatten the one ball of dough by hand and put it through the plain rollers on the widest setting of the pasta maker. Lightly dust the dough with flour as needed. Fold it into thirds and repeat the rolling and folding 8 to 10 times until the dough is smooth and elastic.

Kneading the dough in the pasta maker.

ROLLING

Reduce the space between the rollers by 1 setting. Continue rolling dough through the pasta maker and reducing the space between the rollers, omitting folding into thirds. The sheets of dough will become thinner and longer; cut them in half crosswise for easier handling. Roll the dough until it is about 1/16 inch thick or to the desired thickness, depending on the type of pasta you are making. Place the sheets of dough on lightly floured, dry cloth towels. Let them rest uncovered 15 minutes. Repeat with the remaining balls of dough.

CUTTING

Put sheets of dough through the desired cutting rollers. Spread the cut pieces on a dry cloth towel or over a wooden dowel. Let them stand uncovered 15 to 30 minutes before cooking or 3 to 4 hours to dry completely before storing.

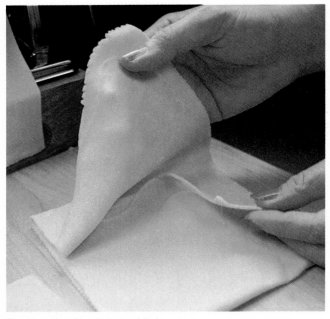

Folding the dough into thirds.

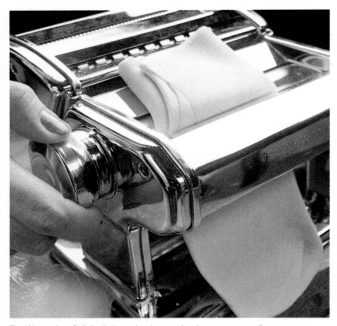

Rolling the folded dough through the pasta maker.

Cutting the dough with the pasta maker.

Drying the dough.

With A Food Processor or Dough Hook

MIXING & KNEADING

If you're using a food processor, insert the metal blade. Place all the ingredients in the processor container. Process about 1 minute until the mixture pulls away from the sides of the container. Remove the dough from the container.

If you're using an electric mixer with a dough hook, place all the ingredients in the large mixer bowl. Beat about 5 minutes on medium speed, occasionally scraping the sides and bottom of the bowl. Remove the dough from the bowl.

If rolling by hand, knead the dough until it is smooth and elastic, about 1 minute, adding more flour if needed. Divide the dough into 3 or 4 balls and place them in a plastic bag to prevent them from drying out. Let them rest in the plastic bag about 30 minutes so the dough will be easier to handle. If you have a pasta maker you can roll 1 ball of the dough immediately. Flatten it slightly by hand and put it through the plain rollers on the widest setting of the pasta maker. Lightly dust the dough with flour as needed. Fold the dough into thirds and repeat the rolling and folding 4 to 5 times until it is smooth and pliable. Repeat with the remaining balls of dough.

ROLLING

Roll out the dough by hand, page 10, or continue rolling through the pasta maker following the directions on page 12.

CUTTING

Cut the dough by hand, page 11, or in the pasta maker, page 12.

Store pasta in airtight containers.

How To Store Pasta

Pasta is dehydrated food so it keeps well and is easy to store. Thoroughly dried pasta should feel smooth and will snap clean when dry. It should not crumble.

If you don't cook fresh homemade pasta immediately, dry it well and store it in tightly covered containers in a cool, dry place.

Pasta you buy may be kept in a cool, dry place up to 1 year. Once the package is opened, store it in a covered glass or plastic container.

Campers find pasta is a practical food to pack because it doesn't need refrigeration and is lightweight and easy to pack.

Plain Pasta

Detailed instructions for using a pasta maker, food processor or dough hook are on pages 11 to 13.

3 cups all-purpose or unbleached flour   **1 teaspoon salt**
3/4 cup plus 2 tablespoons water

Place flour in a mound on a large flat surface. Make a well in the center. Add water and salt. Using a fork, gently start to work flour from the side of the well into the liquid mixture. Continue until dough becomes sticky and difficult to work with the fork. Knead by hand to make a rough-looking dough. Let dough rest 10 minutes. Knead dough until most of the flour is used and dough is smooth and elastic, about 10 minutes. Divide dough into 3 or 4 balls and place balls in a plastic bag; set aside to rest 30 minutes before rolling by hand. Roll out 1 ball at a time to desired thickness and cut into desired shape and width. Makes about 6 servings.

Variations

Beet Pasta: Drain 1 (8-ounce) can cooked sliced beets. Puree in blender with 1 tablespoon vegetable oil. Make a well in 2-1/2 cups all-purpose or unbleached flour. Spoon beet puree into well. Add 1 teaspoon salt. Continue as directed for Plain Pasta. Makes about 4 servings.

Broccoli Pasta: Cook 10 ounces frozen chopped broccoli; drain. Puree in blender with 1 room temperature, large egg. Make a well in 2-1/2 cups all-purpose or unbleached flour. Spoon broccoli puree into well. Add 1 teaspoon salt. Continue as directed for Plain Pasta. Makes about 4 servings.

Egg Noodle Pasta: Make a well in 2-1/4 cups all-purpose or unbleached flour. Break 3 room temperature, large eggs into the well. Add 1 teaspoon salt. Beat mixture in the well with a fork about 10 strokes before working in flour. Continue as directed for Plain Pasta. Makes about 4 servings.

Egg Pasta: Make a well in 3 cups all-purpose, unbleached, semolina or whole-wheat flour. Break 4 room temperature, large eggs into the well. Add 1 tablespoon vegetable oil, 1 tablespoon water and 1/2 teaspoon salt. Beat mixture in the well with a fork about 10 strokes before working in flour. Continue as directed for Plain Pasta. Makes about 6 servings.

Lemon Pasta: Make a well in 2 cups all-purpose or unbleached flour. Add 1/3 cup lemon juice, grated peel of 2 lemons and 1/2 teaspoon salt to the well. Continue as directed for Plain Pasta. Makes about 4 servings.

Onion Pasta: Make a well in 2-1/2 cups all-purpose or unbleached flour. Break 4 room temperature, large eggs into the well. Add 2 tablespoons vegetable oil and 1 (1-1/4-ounce) package dry onion soup mix. Beat mixture in the well with a fork about 10 strokes before working in flour. Continue as directed for Plain Pasta. Makes about 4 servings.

Orange Pasta: Make a well in 2 cups all-purpose or unbleached flour. Drop 1 room temperature, large egg yolk into the well. Add 1 (6-ounce) can thawed, frozen orange juice concentrate. Beat mixture in the well with a fork about 10 strokes before working in flour. Continue as directed for Plain Pasta. Makes about 4 servings.

Pineapple Pasta: Make a well in 2-1/4 cups all-purpose or unbleached flour. Gently add 1 (6-ounce) can thawed, frozen pineapple juice concentrate and 1/4 cup sugar to the well. Beat mixture in the well with a fork about 10 strokes before working in flour. Continue as directed for Plain Pasta. Makes about 4 servings.

Egg Equivalents

When preparing your own pasta dough, it's important to use the right amount of eggs. These recipes call for large eggs, but sometimes they may not be available. If you can't find large eggs, refer to this table and use the appropriate number or amount of medium or small eggs.

LARGE EGGS		MEDIUM EGGS		SMALL EGGS	SPOON OR CUP MEASURE
1	or	1		—	= about 3 tablespoons
2	or	2	or	3	= 1/4 cup plus 1 tablespoon
3	or	4	or	4	= 1/2 cup plus 2 tablespoons

Semolina Flour Pasta: Make a well in 2 cups semolina flour. Add 1/2 cup plus 3 tablespoons water, 2 tablespoons vegetable oil and 1 teaspoon salt to the well. Continue as directed for Plain Pasta. Makes about 4 servings.

Spicy Italian Pasta: Make a well in 2 cups all-purpose or unbleached flour. Break 1 room temperature, large egg into well. Add 1/4 cup water, 2 tablespoons vinegar, 1 tablespoon vegetable oil and 1 (.06-ounce) package dry Italian salad dressing mix. Beat mixture in the well with a fork about 10 strokes before working in flour. Continue as directed for Plain Pasta. Makes 3 to 4 dozen chips.

Spinach Pasta: Cook 10 ounces of fresh or frozen spinach; drain. Puree in blender with 1 room temperature, large egg. Make a well in 3 cups all-purpose or unbleached flour. Break another room temperature, large egg into well. Add 1-1/2 teaspoons salt. Beat mixture in the well with a fork about 10 strokes. Add spinach puree and beat before working in the flour. Continue as directed for Plain Pasta. Makes about 6 servings.

Whole-Wheat Pasta: Make a well in 2 cups sifted whole-wheat flour. Break 2 room temperature, large eggs into the well. Add 2 to 3 tablespoons water, 1 tablespoon vegetable oil and 1 teaspoon salt. Beat mixture in the well with a fork about 10 strokes before working in flour. Continue as directed for Plain Pasta. Makes about 4 servings.

Zucchini Pasta: Cook 10 ounces cubed fresh zucchini in 1/2 cup boiling water until tender; drain. Puree in blender with 1 room temperature, large egg and 1 tablespoon vegetable oil. Make a well in 4 cups all-purpose or unbleached flour. Break another room temperature, large egg into well. Add 2 teaspoons sugar and 1 teaspoon salt. Beat mixture in the well with a fork about 10 strokes. Add zucchini puree and beat before working in the flour. Continue as directed for Plain Pasta. Makes about 8 servings.

Spaetzle

For added flavor, cook these dumplings in chicken broth.

3 eggs
3 cups all-purpose or unbleached flour
1 cup water

1 teaspoon salt
2 qts. chicken broth

In a large bowl, beat eggs, flour, water and salt until thick and smooth. In a large pot or Dutch oven, bring both to a boil. Place 1/4 of the dough on a small, wet chopping board. Flatten with hands to 1/4 inch thick. Dip a sharp knife in a glass of water. Cut 2-1/2" x 1/4" strips of dough. *Carefully* push strips 1 at a time off the board into boiling broth. Repeat with remaining dough. Do not crowd dumplings in broth. Dumplings will be firm and float when cooked. Remove with a slotted spoon. Keep warm in a deep dish while cooking remaining dumplings. Makes 6 to 8 servings.

How To Make Spaetzle

1/Place 1/4 of the dough on wet chopping board. Wet your hand and press dough to flatten 1/4 inch thick. Dip a sharp knife into water and cut strips of dough. Push strips off the board directly into boiling water or broth.

2/Do not crowd spaetzle while cooking. When done, dumplings will be firm and float to the top. Remove them with a slotted spoon.

Bavarian Spaetzle

Make these tiny dumplings for Deutsch Meatballs With Spaetzle, page 133.

2 eggs	Freshly grated nutmeg to taste
1/3 cup water	2 qts. water
1-1/2 cups all-purpose or unbleached flour	2 teaspoons salt
1/2 teaspoon salt	2 tablespoons butter

Beat eggs in a medium bowl. Add 1/3 cup water, flour, 1/2 teaspoon salt and grated nutmeg. Beat until thick and smooth. In a large pot or Dutch oven bring 2 quarts water and remaining 2 teaspoons salt to a boil. Using a 1/8 teaspoon or 1/4 teaspoon measure, pinch off pieces of dough and drop dough into boiling water. Cook 1/4 of the dough at a time. Dumplings will be firm and float when cooked. Remove with a slotted spoon. Keep warm while cooking remaining dumplings. In a small skillet, cook butter over medium heat until dark brown. Pour over spaetzle; toss and serve immediately. Makes 4 servings.

Pasta Flatbread *Photo on page 27.*

Use this variation of the Chinese flatbread to make the sandwiches on page 61.

3 cups all-purpose flour	4 tablespoons vegetable oil
1 teaspoon salt	1 tablespoon butter, melted
1 cup boiling water	

In a large bowl, mix flour and salt. Slowly add boiling water and 3 tablespoons oil. Blend with a fork. Shape dough into a ball. On a lightly floured board, knead 7 minutes until dough is smooth. Shape into an 18-inch roll. Slice 1-inch thick to make 18 pieces. Wrap sliced roll in foil to prevent dough from drying out. Combine remaining 1 tablespoon oil and butter in a small bowl. On a lightly floured board, roll out 2 pieces of dough into two 4-inch circles. Brush tops well with oil mixture. Placing oiled sides together, roll out to an 8-inch circle, being careful not to wrinkle dough. Place a lightly oiled 10-inch skillet over medium heat. Cook flatbread 2 to 3 minutes on each side, until it has blisters and is light brown. Separate the 2 layers of flatbread. Lightly brown uncooked sides in skillet. Wrap in foil to keep warm. Repeat with remaining pieces of dough. Serve hot or wrap in foil and refrigerate or freeze. To reheat, pour water 1 inch deep into a large pot and place 2 or 3 empty custard cups in bottom of pot. Place breads on a pie plate on top of custard cups. Cover and bring to a boil; simmer 10 minutes. Makes 18 flatbreads.

Won Ton Skins

You can make egg roll wrappers from this recipe—just make the squares larger.

2 cups all-purpose or unbleached flour
1 teaspoon salt

2 eggs
1/2 cup plus 1 tablespoon water

Mix flour and salt in a medium bowl. Make a well in the center of the flour. Break eggs into the well. Add water. With a fork, beat eggs and water about 10 strokes. Gently start to work flour and salt from the side of the well into the egg mixture until dough becomes sticky and difficult to work with the fork. Let dough rest 10 minutes. Knead until dough is smooth and elastic. Cover and let rest 30 minutes. Divide the dough into 3 equal portions. Place 2 portions in a plastic bag. On a floured surface, roll out the third portion almost paper-thin to a 12" x 12" sheet. With a knife or pastry wheel, cut sixteen 3-inch squares for won ton skins or four 6-inch squares for egg roll wrappers. Sprinkle a little cornstarch between the squares, stack and place in a plastic bag. Repeat with remaining dough. Makes 40 to 50 won ton skins or about 12 egg roll wrappers.

Raw Carrot Pasta

You'll need either a blender or food processor to make this one.

2 cups diced raw carrots
3 large eggs, room temperature
1 tablespoon vegetable oil

2-1/2 to 3 cups semolina flour
1 teaspoon salt

In a blender container, combine carrots, eggs and oil. Puree about 30 seconds. Place flour in a mound on a large flat surface. Make a well in the center. Gently add carrot puree and salt. With a fork, gently start to work flour from the side of the well into the puree. Continue until dough becomes sticky and difficult to work with the fork. Knead by hand to make a rough looking dough. Let dough rest 10 minutes. If working by hand, knead dough until most of the flour is used and dough is smooth and elastic, about 10 minutes. Roll out by hand after dough rests in a plastic bag 30 minutes. If using pasta machine, you can finish kneading the dough and roll out immediately. Whichever method you use, divide dough into 3 balls. Roll out 1 ball at a time into desired thickness and cut into desired shape and width. Makes about 6 servings.

Variation

To make with food processor: Insert the metal blade in processor. Place carrots, eggs and oil in container. Process until carrots are pureed, about 30 seconds. Add 2-1/2 cups flour and salt. Process until mixture leaves sides of container and forms a ball. Add remaining flour if needed. Remove dough and knead by hand until dough is smooth and elastic, about 1 minute. Add more flour if needed.

Use whole-wheat flour to replace the white all-purpose flour in any pasta recipe.

Cooked Carrot Pasta

Delightful cornucopias to fill with creamed chicken or ham.

2 to 2-1/4 cups all-purpose or
   unbleached flour
1/2 cup water
2 cups sliced raw carrots
1 tablespoon sugar

1 large egg, room temperature
1 tablespoon vegetable oil
1 tablespoon water
1/2 teaspoon salt
Melted butter

Spread flour in a 13" x 9" baking pan. Place baking pan in cold oven. Set temperature control at 400°F (205°C). Toast 15 minutes until flour is light bolden brown, stirring occasionally; set aside. Turn off oven. In a 1-quart saucepan, bring 1/2 cup water to a boil. Add carrots and sugar. Cover and cook 10 minutes over medium heat. Drain well. Puree carrot mixture in blender with egg, oil, 1 tablespoon water and salt. Place toasted flour in a mound on a large flat surface. Make a well in the center. Spoon pureed mixture into the well. With a fork gently start to work flour from the side of the well into the carrot mixture. Continue until dough becomes sticky and difficult to work with the fork. Knead by hand to form a rough-looking dough. Let rest 10 minutes. Knead dough until most of the flour is used and dough is smooth and elastic, about 10 minutes, adding more flour if needed. If rolling by hand, place dough in a plastic bag and let rest 30 minutes. If using pasta machine, you can roll out immediately. Whichever method you use, divide dough into 9 equal parts. Preheat oven to 350°F (175°C). Butter a baking sheet. Roll out each piece of dough to a 5-inch square about 1/8 inch thick. Trim edges with pastry cutter. Set trimmings aside. Form cornu-copias by bringing 2 opposite corners of each pasta square up and overlapping, leaving a wide opening at 1 end and little or no opening at the other end. Fold edge of wide opening over to form a rim. Gently turn up the narrow end to make a small curl. Place cornucopia on the buttered baking sheet with a small crumbled piece of foil holding up the curled end. Crumble a larger piece of foil and place it inside the cornucopia to prevent it from collapsing. Make the 10th cornucopia from dough trimmings. Brush each cornucopia with melted butter. Bake 5 minutes in preheated oven. Cool on wire rack before filling. Cornucopias may be prepared a day ahead. Makes 10 cornucopias.

Variation

Cooked Carrot Pasta may be made into any noodle shape, cooked in boiling water and served with butter. Makes 4 to 5 servings.

If pasta dough flakes and is difficult to handle, work a few drops of water into the dough.

Manicotti

Fill these delicate noodle-crepes with any cheese or meat and vegetable filling.

3 eggs
3/4 cup water
1/2 teaspoon salt

1 tablespoon vegetable oil
3/4 cup all-purpose or unbleached flour
Vegetable oil for frying

Beat eggs in a medium bowl. Add water, salt and 1 tablespoon oil. Blend in flour. Heat a 6-inch crepe pan or skillet over medium-high heat. Lightly brush pan with oil. Pour 2 tablespoons batter in center of pan. Tilt pan quickly to coat bottom of pan evenly. Cook 35 to 45 seconds or until crepe is dry and firm in the center; crepes should be golden but not browned. Do not turn. Remove and stack between waxed paper. If necessary, brush pan with oil every second crepe. Repeat until all crepes are made. Makes about 16 crepes.

Sweet Dessert Manicotti

Lacy crepes will charm your guests. Try the recipes on pages 145, 152, 156 and 157.

3 eggs
3/4 cup water
2 tablespoons sugar

Dash salt
3/4 cup all-purpose or unbleached flour
Soft butter

Beat eggs in a medium bowl. Add water, sugar and salt. Blend in flour. Heat a 6-inch crepe pan or skillet over medium-high heat. Lightly brush pan with butter. Pour 2 tablespoons batter in center of pan. Tilt quickly to coat bottom of pan evenly. Cook about 35 to 45 seconds or until crepe is dry and firm in the center. Crepes should be golden brown. Turn and cook until second side is golden brown. Remove and stack between waxed paper. Brush pan with butter after each crepe. Repeat until all crepes are made. Makes about 16 crepes.

Chocolate Dessert Pasta

Do not make this recipe in your food processor. The dough needs to be worked by hand.

1 cup all-purpose flour
1 cup unsweetened cocoa powder

1 cup powdered sugar
2 large eggs, room temperature

Spread flour in a 9" x 2" baking dish. Place in cold oven. Set temperature control at 400°F (205°C). Toast about 15 minutes until flour is light golden brown, stirring occasionally. Place toasted flour, cocoa and powdered sugar in a mound on a large flat surface. Mix together. Make a well in the center. Break eggs into the well. With a fork, beat eggs about 15 strokes. Gently start to work some of the flour mixture from the side of the well into the beaten eggs. Continue until dough becomes sticky and difficult to work with the fork. Knead dough by hand to form a rough-looking ball. Let rest 10 minutes. Knead dough until most of the flour is used and dough is smooth and elastic, about 10 minutes. Place pasta dough in a plastic bag and set aside. Makes enough pasta for Chocolate Cornucopias, Chocolate Covered Cherries and Petite Chocolate Sandwiches, page 146.

Appetizers

Antipasto is the Italian word for appetizer and it means something served before the main course or, literally, before the pasta. Antipasto usually consists of a variety of cheeses, sausage and hot peppers. However, there is no reason to exclude pasta. Do try my version of antipasto. If you serve a pasta appetizer once, it's likely to become a habit!

Mostaccioli forms the basis for two unusual appetizers. Spinach Squares are made by baking spinach and mostaccioli in a custard. In Cheese Combos, four cheeses are combined in a ravioli filling. Both these hearty appetizers can also be served as hors d'oeuvres at a cocktail party where there is no dinner to follow.

Cut Pasta Flatbread, page 17, into small pieces and substitute them for crackers or small cocktail bread. Pasta Flatbread goes well with any spread or dip.

In working with pasta, I developed a new and different-tasting natural snack called *pasta chips!* These original recipes for Spinetta Chips and Snappy Sesame Chips are included in this section.

Menu
Friends—No Invitation Necessary
Spinetta Chips, page 26
Snappy Sesame Chips, page 24
Creamy Onion Dip
Sassy Swiss Spread, page 25
Glazed Ham Balls In Noodle Ring, page 73
Assorted Crisp Relishes
Mixed Nuts
Fresh Fruit Punch

Crab Spread

Succulent crab, cream cheese and mild chili sauce is splendid on Pasta Flatbread, page 17.

1 (8-oz.) pkg. cream cheese, room temperature	1 tablespoon pickle relish, drained
1/2 cup dairy sour cream or plain yogurt	1 (6-oz.) pkg. crab, drained, flaked
1 green onion, minced	1/2 cup chili sauce
1 tablespoon minced pimiento, drained	1/4 teaspoon Worcestershire sauce

In a small bowl, beat cream cheese and sour cream or yogurt until smooth. Stir in onion, pimiento and pickle relish. On a platter, shape mixture into a flat mound about 1-inch high. Refrigerate 2 hours. Before serving, sprinkle crab over cheese mixture. In a small bowl, combine chili sauce and Worcestershire sauce. Pour over crab. Makes 1-1/2 cups.

Variation
Substitute 6 ounces cooked chopped shrimp for the crab.

Shrimp Egg Rolls

If you prefer to make your own egg roll wrappers, follow the Won Ton Skins recipe, page 18.

1 tablespoon vegetable oil
2 cups frozen cooked shrimp, finely chopped
    (6 oz.)
1/3 cup sliced green onion
1/2 cup chopped fresh or canned bean sprouts,
    well-drained
1 tablespoon minced water chestnuts
1 tablespoon soy sauce

1 teaspoon grated fresh ginger root
1/4 teaspoon salt
1/8 teaspoon white pepper
1 egg, slightly beaten
10 egg roll wrappers, 5 to 6 inches square
Oil for deep-frying
Sweet-Sour Sauce, see below

Sweet-Sour Sauce:
1/2 cup firmly packed brown sugar
1-1/2 tablespoons cornstarch
1-1/2 cups pineapple juice

1/4 cup red wine vinegar
2 tablespoons soy sauce

In a wok or large skillet, heat vegetable oil over medium heat. Stir-fry or sauté shrimp and green onion until golden, 2 to 3 minutes. Add bean sprouts, water chestnuts, soy sauce, ginger root, salt and white pepper. Heat 1 minute. Remove from heat. Set aside to cool. Stir beaten egg into shrimp mixture. Spread 2 tablespoons filling along 1 side of each egg roll wrapper. Fold over end of wrapper and roll up jelly-roll fashion. Dip fingers into water and moisten free edge of each egg roll. Using fingers, press edge to seal. Cover completed egg rolls with plastic wrap to prevent drying. Heat deep-frying oil to 365°F (185°C). At this temperature, a 1-inch cube of bread will turn golden brown in 50 seconds. Deep-fry egg rolls in hot oil until surface is crisp, bubbly and golden, 3 to 4 minutes. Serve with Sweet-Sour Sauce. Makes 10 egg rolls.

Sweet-Sour Sauce:
Combine all ingredients in a 1-quart saucepan. Cook over medium heat until sauce is thickened and clear, about 10 minutes. Set aside to cool. Makes about 2 cups.

Variation
Substitute 2 cups finely chopped cooked chicken or turkey for cooked shrimp.

Macaroni-Bean Relish

Also a perfect cold, slightly tangy, side dish.

3 cups water
1/2 teaspoon salt
1 teaspoon vegetable oil
1/2 cup macaroni shells, uncooked (2 oz.)
1 (16-oz.) can red kidney beans, drained
3/4 cup chopped pimiento-stuffed olives

1/2 cup minced onion
1/4 cup plain yogurt
1/4 cup mayonnaise-style salad dressing
1 teaspoon red wine vinegar
Garlic salt to taste

Bring water to a rapid boil in a heavy 2-quart saucepan. Add salt and oil. Gradually add shells, being sure water continues to boil. Cook shells uncovered until tender but firm, stirring occasionally. Drain. Rinse with cold water. Drain again. In a medium bowl with a tight lid, mix macaroni shells, kidney beans, olives and onion. In a small bowl, combine yogurt, salad dressing, vinegar and garlic salt. Pour yogurt mixture over relish and toss lightly. Cover tightly. Refrigerate 1/2 hour or overnight before serving. Makes about 3 cups.

How To Make Shrimp Egg Rolls

1/In a wok or large skillet, stir-fry shrimp and green onions by tossing and turning in hot oil.

2/Spread filling along one side of egg roll wrapper, leaving about 1/4-inch on each end. Fold over ends of skin and roll like a jelly roll. Seal seam of roll with a little water. Repeat with each skin.

Spinach Squares

Mostaccioli base is covered with a spinach custard.

1-1/2 lbs. fresh spinach or 2 (10-oz.) pkgs.
   frozen spinach, thawed
1/2 teaspoon salt
2 tablespoons vegetable oil
1-1/2 cups chopped onion
1 cup feta cheese, crumbled fine
1/4 cup chopped fresh parsley
1 teaspoon dried dill weed
1/2 teaspoon dried mint
1/2 teaspoon salt

1/4 teaspoon black pepper
5 eggs, well-beaten
4 cups water
1/2 teaspoon salt
1 teaspoon vegetable oil
1-1/2 cups mostaccioli, uncooked
1 egg, slightly beaten
1/4 cup half-and-half
2 tablespoons butter

Place spinach in a colander. Sprinkle with 1/2 teaspoon salt. Let stand 1/2 hour. Butter an 11" x 7" baking dish; set aside. Squeeze spinach to remove excess water. Heat 2 tablespoons oil in a medium skillet. Sauté onion in oil until golden. In a large bowl, combine spinach, sautéed onions, feta cheese, parsley, dill, mint, 1/2 teaspoon salt and pepper. Add 5 well-beaten eggs. Mix thoroughly; set aside. Bring water to a rapid boil in a heavy 2-quart saucepan. Add 1/2 teaspoon salt and 1 teaspoon oil. Gradually add mostaccioli, being sure water continues to boil. Cook mostaccioli uncovered until tender but firm, stirring occasionally. Drain. In a medium bowl, combine 1 slightly beaten egg, half-and-half and cooked mostaccioli. Arrange mostaccioli mixture evenly in bottom of prepared baking dish. Carefully spoon spinach mixture over top of mostaccioli mixture. Dot with butter. Place baking dish in cold oven. Set temperature control at 350°F (175°C). Bake 45 minutes. Cut in twenty-four 1-1/2-inch squares. Serve hot or warm. Makes 24 squares.

Snappy Sesame Chips *Photo on page 27.*

Semolina flour is a protein-rich, creamy-colored, granular, duram-wheat flour.

1-1/2 cups semolina flour
2 large eggs, room temperature
2 tablespoons honey

3/4 cup sesame seeds
2 teaspoons salt
Oil for deep-frying

Place semolina flour in a mound on a large flat surface. Make a well in the center. Break eggs into the well. Add honey, sesame seeds and salt. With a fork, beat eggs in the well with honey, seeds and salt about 15 strokes. Gently start to work the flour from the side of the well into the beaten egg mixture. Continue until dough becomes sticky and difficult to work with the fork. Knead by hand to make a rough-looking dough. Let dough rest 10 minutes. If working by hand, knead dough until most of the flour is used and dough is smooth and elastic, about 10 minutes. Roll out by hand after dough rests in a plastic bag 30 minutes. If using pasta machine, finish kneading dough and roll out immediately. Whichever method you use, divide dough into 3 balls. Roll out 1 ball at a time 1/16 inch thick. Sprinkle lightly with flour; let rest 15 minutes on a lightly floured cloth towel. Cut into 1" x 3/4" rectangles. Repeat with remaining balls of dough. Preheat oil to 365°F (185°C). At this temperature, a 1-inch cube of bread turns golden brown in 50 seconds. Deep-fry chips until golden, 3 to 5 seconds. Do not overcook. Drain on paper towels. Cool. Makes about 12 dozen chips.

Sassy Swiss Spread *Photo on page 27.*

Serve a bowl of this chilled spread with triangles of Pasta Flatbread, page 17.

1/2 lb. Swiss cheese, coarsely shredded
1 tablespoon minced chives
2 tablespoons chopped green pepper
3 tablespoons chopped
   pimiento-stuffed olives

1 small tomato, finely chopped (1/2 cup)
1/2 cup mayonnaise-style salad dressing
1/4 teaspoon salt
Few drops Tabasco sauce

In a medium bowl, combine all ingredients. Refrigerate until serving time. Makes 2 cups.

Zucchini Thimbles

Risino, *tiny rice-like pasta, is usually used in soup.*

10 small zucchini, 4 to 5 inches long
1 cup boiling water
Tiny Rice Filling, see below

6 tablespoons water
2 tablespoons tomato sauce
1/4 teaspoon salt

Tiny Rice Filling:
2 tablespoons vegetable oil
1/2 cup minced onion
1/4 cup risino
1-1/4 cups water
1 small tomato, peeled, diced
1/4 cup minced fresh parsley
2 tablespoons reserved zucchini pulp

1 tablespoon tomato sauce
1/2 teaspoon salt
1/4 teaspoon dried dill weed
1/8 teaspoon dried oregano
1/8 teaspoon dried mint
Black pepper to taste

Cook uncut zucchini in 1 cup boiling water 5 minutes. Drain. Cool slightly. Cut cooked zucchini into 1/2-inch to 3/4-inch slices. Using a 1/4 teaspoon measuring spoon, carefully scoop out centers, leaving 1/4-inch thick shells. Reserve 2 tablespoons finely chopped pulp for filling. Place zucchini shells in a small baking dish. Prepare Tiny Rice Filling. Spoon filling into each shell. In a small saucepan oven medium heat, blend 6 tablespoons water, tomato sauce and salt. Bring to a boil. Pour into bottom of baking dish around stuffed zucchini shells. Cover and place in cold oven. Set temperature control at 350°F (175°C). Bake 30 minutes. Serve warm. Makes about 30 appetizers.

Tiny Rice Filling:
Heat oil in a large skillet over medium heat. Sauté onion until golden. Stir in risino; cook about 1 minute. Add water, tomato, parsley, reserved zucchini pulp, tomato sauce, salt, dill, oregano, mint and pepper. Bring to a boil. Cook until liquid is absorbed, 5 to 7 minutes. Remove from heat.

Variation
If using large zucchini, 7 to 8-inches long, slice crosswise 1 inch thick. Scoop out centers of each slice, leaving 1/4-inch shells.

Spinetta Chips

Drop some of these nicely seasoned chips into your fresh salad.

Seasoning Mix, see below
1/2 (10-oz.) pkg. frozen spinach
2 tablespoons boiling water
2 large eggs, room temperature

2 cups semolina flour
1 teaspoon vegetable oil
1 teaspoon warm water
Oil for deep-frying

Seasoning Mix:
1 tablespoon coarse salt
3 tablespoons grated Parmesan cheese
1/2 teaspoon garlic salt

1/2 teaspoon black pepper
1/2 teaspoon onion salt
1/2 teaspoon dried oregano

Prepare Seasoning Mix; set aside. In a 1-quart saucepan, place spinach in 2 tablespoons boiling water over medium heat. Cover and reduce heat. Cook 7 minutes. Drain well. Puree cooked spinach in blender with 1 of the eggs. Place semolina flour in a mound on a large flat surface. Make a well in the center. Break remaining egg into well. Add pureed spinach, vegetable oil, 1 teaspoon warm water and Seasoning Mix. With a fork, beat mixture in the well about 15 strokes. Gently start to work the flour from the side of the well into the spinach mixture. Continue until dough becomes sticky and difficult to work with a fork. Knead by hand to make a rough-looking dough. Let dough rest 10 minutes. If working by hand, knead dough until most of the flour is used and dough is smooth and elastic, about 10 minutes. Let dough rest in a plastic bag 30 minutes before rolling out on a lightly floured surface. If using pasta machine, you can finish kneading the dough and roll out immediately. Whichever method you use, divide dough into 3 balls. Roll out 1 ball at a time 1/16 inch thick. Sprinkle dough lightly with flour. Let rest 15 minutes on a lightly floured dry cloth towel. With a knife, cut dough into 1" x 3/4" rectangles. Repeat with remaining balls of dough. Preheat deep-frying oil to 365°F (185°C). At this temperature, a 1-inch cube of bread will turn golden brown in 50 seconds. Deep-fry chips until golden, 3 to 5 seconds. Do not overcook. Drain on paper towels. Cool. Makes about 12 dozen chips.

Seasoning Mix:
Mix all ingredients in a small bowl.

On the glass plate, from the top, clockwise: Snappy Sesame Chips, page 24; Pasta Flatbread, page 17, and Spinetta Chips, above. Sassy Swiss Spread, page 25, is in the glass bowl.

Cheese Combos

Step-by-step how-to photographs for making ravioli are on page 70.

Cheese Filling, see below	1 egg, slightly beaten
3 cups all-purpose flour	1/2 teaspoon salt
3/4 cup milk	Oil for deep-frying
1/4 cup water	

Cheese Filling:

1 (8-oz.) pkg. cream cheese, softened	1 teaspoon minced fresh parsley
4 eggs	1/8 teaspoon salt
1/2 carton ricotta cheese (8 oz.)	Dill weed to taste
4 oz. feta cheese	Onion salt to taste
1/4 cup grated Parmesan cheese	Garlic salt to taste

Prepare Cheese Filling; set aside. Place flour in a large bowl. Make a well in the center. Pour milk, water, egg and salt into the well. With a fork, beat milk mixture in the well about 15 strokes. Stir in flour to form a rough-looking ball of dough. Place on a lightly floured surface. Knead until dough is smooth and elastic, 10 minutes. Divide dough into 3 equal balls. Place balls in a plastic bag to prevent drying. Let rest 10 minutes. Remove 1 ball of dough from bag; divide into 2 equal-size pieces. Roll the pieces into two 13" x 5" rectangles, 1/8 inch thick. On 1 of the rectangles, place Cheese Filling by rounded teaspoonfuls in 2 rows of 6 mounds each. Mounds should be about 2 inches apart. Cover with the second pasta rectangle. Use your fingers to press around each mound of filling. With a pastry cutter, cut between the mounds to make 12 squares. If using a knife to cut between the squares, press with a fork to seal edges after cutting. Repeat dividing, rolling and filling with remaining 2 balls of dough. **If using a ravioli form**, place 1 pasta rectangle over the indented tray. Place plastic insert onto dough to make indentations. Remove insert. Place about 1 rounded teaspoon filling into each indentation. Place another pasta rectangle over the top. With a rolling pin, roll firmly back and forth over fluted edges on the indented tray to trim off excess dough and cut into squares. Remove individual squares from tray, checking edges for poor seal. Repeat with remaining 2 rolls of pasta dough. Place cut combos on a lightly floured cloth towel to dry, about 1 hour. In a deep pot, heat oil to 375°F (190°C). At this temperature, a 1-inch cube of bread will turn golden brown in 40 seconds. Deep-fry combos until golden, 30 seconds. Drain on paper towels. Serve hot. Makes 36 to 40 appetizers.

Cheese Filling:

In a large bowl, beat cream cheese until light and fluffy. Add eggs, ricotta cheese and feta cheese; mix thoroughly. Blend in remaining ingredients.

Hot Tuna Puffs

Cut the remaining dough into noodles or make Cheese Combos, opposite.

Tuna Fish Filling, see below
1/2 Raw Carrot Pasta dough, page 18

Oil for deep-frying

Tuna Fish Filling:

1 (10-oz.) can tuna fish, flaked, drained
2 tablespoons minced celery
1 tablespoon minced onion

1/4 teaspoon lemon juice
1/8 teaspoon salt
Black pepper to taste

Prepare Tuna Fish Filling; set aside. Divide dough into 4 equal balls. If using a pasta machine, roll out immediately. If rolling out by hand, place dough in a plastic bag; let rest 1 hour. On a lightly floured surface, roll out 2 balls of dough into two 13" x 5" rectangles, 1/8 inch thick. On 1 of the rectangles, place Tuna Fish Filling by rounded teaspoonfuls in 2 rows of 6 mounds each. Mounds should be about 2 inches apart. Cover with the second pasta rectangle. Use your fingers to press around each mound of filling. With a pastry cutter, cut between the mounds to make 12 puffs. If using a knife to cut between the squares, press with a fork to seal edges after cutting. Repeat with remaining 2 balls of dough. **If using a ravioli form**, place 1 pasta rectangle over the indented tray. Place plastic insert onto dough to make indentations. Remove insert. Place about 1 rounded teaspoon filling into each indentation. Place another pasta rectangle over the top. With a rolling pin, roll firmly back and forth over fluted edges on the indented tray to trim off excess dough and cut into squares. Remove individual squares from tray, checking edges for poor seal. Repeat with remaining 2 rolls of pasta dough. Place cut squares on a lightly floured cloth towel to dry before cooking, about 1 hour. In a heavy deep pot, heat oil to 365°F (185°C). At this temperature, a 1-inch cube of bread will turn golden brown in 50 seconds. Deep-fry puffs until golden, 2 to 3 minutes. Drain on paper towels. Serve hot. Makes about 35 puffs.

Tuna Fish Filling:
In a medium bowl, combine all ingredients.

Add interest to an appetizer tray: Fill cooked jumbo pasta shells with a fish or seafood mixture and arrange on a tray with other appetizers. These filled shells can be made early in the day and refrigerated.

Seafood Shells

Pickles, olives and chili sauce give these stuffed shells an antipasto flavor.

1 (7-oz.) can white tuna fish, drained, flaked
1 (4-1/2-oz.) can medium shrimp, drained
1/2 cup pearl onions, cooked
1/2 cup chopped sweet mixed pickles
1/2 cup sliced pimiento-stuffed olives
1 (12-oz.) jar chili sauce
2 tablespoons prepared horseradish

1/2 teaspoon Worcestershire sauce
Tabasco sauce to taste
2 qts. water
1-1/2 teaspoons salt
12 jumbo macaroni shells, uncooked
Parsley sprigs for garnish
Bibb lettuce leaves

In a large bowl, toss tuna fish, shrimp, onions, pickles and olives. In a small bowl, mix chili sauce, horseradish, Worcestershire sauce and Tabasco sauce. Gently fold into seafood mixture. Cover and refrigerate while preparing shells. Bring water to a rapid boil in a heavy 4-quart saucepan. Add salt. Gradually add shells, being sure water continues to boil. Cook shells uncovered until tender but quite firm, stirring occasionally. With a slotted spoon, remove shells from water. Invert shells on a dry cloth towel; drain 5 minutes. Fill with chilled seafood mixture. Serve immediately or cover with plastic wrap and refrigerate several hours before serving. Garnish each shell with a sprig of parsley. Serve on lettuce leaves. Makes 12 shells.

Sauerkraut Ravioli

Italians call meat-filled round ravioli agnolotti.

1 egg, slightly beaten
1 cup water
3 tablespoons vegetable oil
1 teaspoon salt

3 cups all-purpose flour
Vegetable oil for dough
Sauerkraut Filling, see below
Oil for deep-frying

Sauerkraut Filling:
2 (1-lb.) cans sauerkraut, drained
1 cup chopped onion

6 tablespoons butter

In a large bowl, combine egg, water, 3 tablespoons oil and salt. Stir in flour, making a stiff dough. Let dough rest 5 minutes. Knead until smooth, 10 minutes. Brush top lightly with vegetable oil. Cover and let stand 1 hour. Prepare Sauerkraut Filling; set aside. On a lightly floured surface, roll out dough 1/8 inch thick. With a biscuit cutter, cut into 3-inch circles. Stretch each circle slightly with your hands. Place 2 teaspoons Sauerkraut Filling on half of each circle. Fold other half over the filling. Seal edges by crimping with a fork, being careful not to puncture the dough. Appetizers may be made several hours ahead and refrigerated before frying or they may be kept frozen up to 3 months, and thawed before frying. In a heavy deep pot, heat deep-frying oil to 375°F (190°C). At this temperature, a 1-inch cube of bread will turn golden brown in 40 seconds. Deep-fry several ravioli at a time until golden, 2 minutes. Drain on paper towels. Serve at once. Makes about 48 appetizers.

Sauerkraut Filling:
In a large bowl, combine all ingredients.

Soups

Soup, like pasta has universal appeal. Serve both in the same bowl and your reputation as a fabulous cook will be established before you know it!

Generally speaking, soups may be divided into three basic groups: thin soups such as consomme, bouillon or broth; light and delicate cream soups, and hearty satisfying soups that are usually served as a main dish.

Pasta used in soups is usually small so it can be eaten with a spoon, but the choice of small pasta shapes is quite wide. Just to mention a few, there are circles, tubes, alphabets, sea shells and wheels. You can also break spaghetti or vermicelli into bite-size pieces and add them to soups.

In general, add 2 cups cooked noodles or macaroni or 2 cups uncooked noodles or 1 cup uncooked macaroni to each 2 quarts of soup.

Uncooked pasta may be added directly to broth or the pasta may be cooked and drained and then added. Add cooked pasta to soup during the last few minutes of the soup's cooking time so the pasta won't be overcooked. If you are serving a delicate consommé and don't want starch to cloud the clarity of the broth, cook the pasta before adding it to the consommé.

Menu
East Meets West
Won Ton Soup, page 33
Shrimp Egg Rolls, page 22
Chinese Stir-Fried Pork, page 51
Hot Thin Egg Pasta Noodles, page 14
Almond Cookies
Tea

Minestrone

Serve this hearty soup with slices of sharp tangy cheese for a complete meal.

5 cups beef broth
1/2 cup tomato sauce
1 cup chopped celery
1/2 cup diced carrot
1 large potato, peeled, chopped
1/3 cup chopped onion
1/2 cup shredded white cabbage

1/3 cup cut green beans
2 tablespoons chopped green pepper
1 large garlic clove, pressed
1/4 teaspoon black pepper
1/3 cup frozen peas
1/2 cup broken spaghetti pieces,
    uncooked (2 oz.)

In a 3-quart saucepan, bring broth and tomato sauce to a boil. Add celery, carrot, potato, onion, cabbage, green beans, green pepper, garlic and black pepper. Reduce heat and simmer 1 hour. Bring to a boil again. Add peas and broken spaghetti pieces. Reduce heat and simmer 15 minutes longer. Makes 8 servings.

Won Ton Soup

Won ton skins may be purchased at some supermarkets and at Oriental specialty shops.

Pork Filling, see below
About 40 (3-inch) Won Ton Skins, page 18
Water for sealing

6 cups chicken broth
1/2 cup snipped parsley for garnish

Pork Filling:
1/4 (10-oz.) pkg. frozen chopped broccoli
1/2 lb. ground or chopped lean pork
2 tablespoons sliced green onion

1-1/2 teaspoons soy sauce
1/2 teaspoon salt
1/2 teaspoon ground ginger

Prepare Pork Filling and Won Ton Skins. Place 1 teaspoon filling in the center of each Won Ton Skin. Moisten edges of skin. Fold 2 opposite corners together, forming a triangle. Seal edges. Pull the right and left corners of folded triangle together and slightly overlap. Moisten overlapping corners and pinch together. Place won tons on a plate and cover with plastic wrap until ready to cook. In a large pot or Dutch oven, bring chicken broth to a boil. Add won tons. Bring to a boil again. Reduce heat and simmer about 6 minutes. Serve won tons and hot broth in warm bowls. Garnish with chopped parsley. Makes 6 to 8 servings.

Pork Filling:
Thaw and drain broccoli. Cook pork in a small skillet, over medium heat until well-done. Drain off fat. Add broccoli, green onion, soy sauce, salt and ginger. Mix well.

Variation
For garnish, substitute 3/4 cup shredded ham and 2 tablespoons finely sliced green onion for 1/2 cup snipped parsley.

Onion Noodle Soup

Delicious served with crusty French bread.

3 tablespoons butter
3 medium onions, thinly sliced
2 tablespoons all-purpose flour
Black pepper to taste

2 (10-1/2-oz.) cans beef broth
2-1/4 cups water
2 cups thin noodles, uncooked (4 oz.)
2 tablespoons grated Parmesan cheese

In a 3-quart saucepan, melt butter over medium heat. Sauté onions until golden, stirring occasionally. Remove onions; set aside. Stir in flour. Cook 2 to 3 minutes. Add pepper. Slowly add broth and water to the flour mixture and bring to a full boil, stirring constantly. Add noodles and sautéed onions. Cover with lid ajar and simmer 5 to 7 minutes. Remove from heat. Add Parmesan cheese. Stir until cheese melts. Serve immediately. Makes 4 to 6 servings.

Egg-Lemon Soup

Take care not to overcook the pasta in this delicately flavored Greek soup.

6 cups chicken broth
3 tablespoons butter
1 teaspoon salt
1/8 teaspoon white pepper

1 cup broken guitar string spaghetti or
   vermicelli cluster, uncooked (2 oz.)
4 eggs
2 tablespoons lemon juice

In a 3-quart saucepan, bring broth, butter, salt and pepper to a boil. Stir spaghetti or vermicelli pieces into broth. Bring to a boil again. Simmer 5 minutes or until pasta is tender. Beat eggs with electric mixer or blender on high speed until thick and light colored, slowly adding lemon juice. Slowly add 1-1/2 cups hot broth to the egg mixture. Gradually pour egg mixture into remaining soup, stirring soup constantly. Serve at once. Makes 6 servings.

Roman Egg Soup

When combining an egg mixture with hot broth, first stir a little of the hot broth into the egg mixture.

6 cups chicken broth
1/2 cup thin noodles, uncooked (1 oz.)
1/4 teaspoon salt
1/8 teaspoon black pepper
1 tablespoon all-purpose flour

2 tablespoons cold water
4 eggs
Grated Parmesan cheese
Minced parsley for garnish

In a 3-quart saucepan, bring broth to a boil. Stir in noodles, salt and pepper. Bring to a boil again. Reduce heat and cook until noodles are tender, 7 minutes. In a small bowl, mix flour and water together. In a medium bowl, beat eggs. Add flour mixture to eggs and beat again. Pour 1 cup hot noodle mixture into egg mixture a little at a time. Gradually add egg mixture to remaining soup. Serve with Parmesan cheese. Garnish with minced parsley. Makes 6 servings.

Quick Vermicelli Soup

Savory herb flavor goes well with seasoned Petite Pasta Puffs, page 38.

4 cups chicken broth
1/4 teaspoon dried dill weed
1/2 teaspoon dried parsley flakes

Black pepper to taste
1/4 cup broken vermicelli cluster, uncooked

In a 2-quart saucepan, bring broth, dill weed, parsley flakes and pepper to a boil. Stir in broken vermicelli. Bring to a boil again. Reduce heat and simmer 4 minutes longer. Serve immediately. Makes 4 servings.

Mint-Yogurt Soup

Blend a little of the hot soup into the yogurt to prevent curdling. Then add the yogurt to the soup.

4 cups water
1 teaspoon salt
1/4 cup small egg bows, uncooked
1/4 cup quick-cooking barley, uncooked

3 tablespoons butter
1-1/2 teaspoons dried mint leaves
1 cup plain yogurt, room temperature

Bring water to a rapid boil in a heavy 2-quart saucepan. Add salt, egg bows and barley, bring to a boil again. Cover and simmer 30 minutes. Melt butter in a small saucepan over medium heat until frothy and golden. Crush dried mint leaves and stir into butter. Add butter mixture to soup. In a small bowl, stir yogurt until smooth. Stir 2 cups hot soup a little at a time into yogurt. Blend yogurt mixture into soup. Keep warm over low heat. Makes 6 to 8 servings.

Garbanzo Soup

Chick-peas are called garbanzos *in Spanish.*

3 tablespoons butter
1/4 cup minced onion
3 cups water
1 (15-oz.) can garbanzos or chick-peas, drained
2 beef bouillon cubes
1/4 teaspoon salt

1/4 teaspoon garlic salt
1/4 teaspoon dried mint leaves
1/8 teaspoon black pepper
1/4 cup soup macaroni, uncooked
Grated Parmesan cheese
Minced parsley for garnish

In a 2-quart saucepan, melt butter over medium heat. Sauté onion until golden. Add water, garbanzos or chick-peas, bouillon cubes, salt, garlic salt, mint leaves and pepper. Bring to a boil. Stir in macaroni. Reduce heat. Cover and simmer 20 minutes. Serve topped with grated Parmesan cheese and garnished with minced parsley. Makes 4 to 6 servings.

Tomato Soup

When you want a quick soup with old-fashioned flavor, try this.

1 (10-3/4-oz.) can tomato soup
2 cups milk
1 tomato, peeled, seeded, chopped

1/2 cup alphabet or soup macaroni,
   cooked, drained
1 tablespoon butter

In a 2-quart saucepan, blend soup and milk. Add tomato. Heat to just under boiling. Stir in alphabet or soup macaroni and butter. Heat through. Serve immediately. Makes 4 servings.

Mini Meatball Soup

Serve this hearty soup as a main dish with crusty bread and a salad.

1/2 lb. ground beef
1/4 cup dry breadcrumbs
1 egg, slightly beaten
2 tablespoons minced fresh parsley
1 tablespoon grated onion
1/2 teaspoon salt
1/8 teaspoon black pepper

3 cups water
2 beef bouillon cubes
1/2 cup tomato sauce
1 tablespoon butter
1/2 cup broken spaghetti, uncooked
  (3/4-inch pieces)

In a medium bowl, mix ground beef, breadcrumbs, egg, parsley, onion, salt and pepper. Form into 16 meatballs. In a 3-quart saucepan, mix water, bouillon cubes, tomato sauce and butter. Bring to a boil. Carefully drop meatballs 1 at a time into the broth. Add spaghetti pieces. Reduce heat. Cover and cook 30 minutes. Serve hot. Makes 4 to 6 servings.

How To Make Mini Meatball Soup

1/To get 16 evenly shaped meatballs, divide meat mixture into 4 equal parts, then divide each part into 4 equal pieces. Gently roll each piece of meat mixture into a ball between the palms of your hands.

2/Place meatballs 1 at a time on a spoon and drop into hot broth. Add broken spaghetti pieces and continue cooking.

Manhattan Clam Chowder

Combine and freeze all but the macaroni and clams. Add them after thawing.

1 slice bacon, chopped
1/2 cup chopped onion
1 cup chopped celery
1/4 cup chopped carrot
1 small potato, peeled, diced
5 cups water
1 (16-oz.) can whole tomatoes,
   undrained, cut up

2 teaspoons salt
1/2 teaspoon dried thyme
1/4 teaspoon black pepper
1 bay leaf
1/4 cup chili macaroni or small macaroni,
   uncooked (1 oz.)
2 (7-oz.) cans chopped clams, drained

In a 3-quart saucepan, fry bacon. Remove bacon and set aside. Sauté onion in bacon drippings. Add celery, carrot and potato. Sauté several minutes. Add water and tomatoes with liquid, salt, thyme, pepper, bay leaf and cooked bacon. Bring to a boil. Reduce heat and cook 30 minutes. Bring to a full boil again. Stir in macaroni. Cook 10 minutes or until macaroni is just tender. Stir in clams; heat through. Makes 8 servings.

Sassy Spinach Soup

To reheat, add a little milk and bring the soup to serving temperature.

1/2 cup chopped onion
1 garlic clove, pressed
2 tablespoons butter or margarine
4 cups water
5 chicken bouillon cubes
1/2 cup noodle flakes or broken thin
   noodles, uncooked
1/2 teaspoon salt

1 (10-oz.) pkg. frozen chopped spinach,
   thawed, drained
3 cups milk
1/2 cup shredded Cheddar cheese (2 oz.)
1/2 cup shredded Swiss cheese (2 oz.)
Black pepper to taste

In a 3-quart saucepan, sauté onion and garlic in butter or margarine until onion is golden, about 5 minutes. Add water and bouillon cubes. Bring to a boil; stir to dissolve bouillon cubes. Add noodle flakes or broken thin noodles slowly being sure water continues to boil. Add salt. Cook uncovered until tender, about 10 minutes, stirring occasionally. Squeeze spinach to remove excess water. Stir spinach into the noodle mixture and cook 5 minutes longer. Stir in milk, Cheddar cheese, Swiss cheese and pepper. Continue stirring over medium-high heat until cheeses are melted. Do not boil. Makes 6 to 8 servings.

If you have leftover cooked noodles, store them in the refrigerator and add them to soup during the last 5 minutes of cooking time.

Petite Pasta Puffs

Float these petite puffs on top of your favorite soup.

1-1/4 to 1-1/2 cups all-purpose flour
2 large eggs, room temperature
2 teaspoons vegetable oil

1-1/2 teaspoons salt
Vegetable oil for deep-frying

Place flour in a mound on a large flat surface. Make a well in the center. Break eggs into well. Add 2 teaspoons vegetable oil and salt. With a fork, beat eggs, oil and salt about 10 strokes. Gently start to work flour from the side of well into the beaten egg mixture. Continue until dough becomes sticky and difficult to work with the fork. Knead by hand until most of the flour is used and dough is smooth and elastic, about 10 minutes. Divide dough in half. Place in a plastic bag. Let dough rest 10 minutes. Roll half the dough by hand or with a pasta machine 1/8 inch thick. With a round 1-inch cutter, cut about 75 circles of dough. Repeat rolling and cutting with remaining dough. In a 4- to 6-quart pot or Dutch oven, heat the oil for deep-frying to 365°F (185°C). At this temperature a 1-inch cube of bread will turn golden brown in 50 to 60 seconds. Deep fry circles of dough 1 minute or until puffed. Drain on paper towels. Store in an airtight container in a cool place or wrap well and freeze. Makes about 150 puffs.

Variations

Seasoned Puffs: Add 1/8 teaspoon each of garlic powder, onion powder and white pepper.
Cheese Puffs: Add 1/3 cup Parmesan cheese.
Herb Puffs: Add 2 tablespoons chopped chives and 1/4 teaspoon Italian herbs.

After-The-Game Chili

Tubetti are small circles of spaghetti that go well in soup or salad.

1-1/2 lbs. lean ground beef
1 medium onion, chopped
1 small garlic clove, pressed
8 cups water
1 (16-oz.) can whole tomatoes, undrained,
    cut up
1 (6-oz.) can tomato paste

1 tablespoon salt
1-1/2 to 2 tablespoons chili powder
1 tablespoon sugar
1/2 teaspoon paprika
1-1/2 cups tubetti, uncooked (5 oz.)
2 (16-oz.) cans dark kidney beans, drained
Grated Cheddar cheese, if desired

Place ground beef, onion and garlic in a large heavy pot or Dutch oven. Break up meat with a fork. Cook over medium heat until meat is browned. Add water, tomatoes with liquid, tomato paste, salt, chili powder, sugar and paprika. Bring to a boil. Reduce heat. Cover and simmer 1-1/2 hours. Bring to a full boil again. Add tubetti and kidney beans, being sure mixture continues to boil. Cover. Reduce heat and simmer 20 minutes longer, stirring often. Sprinkle with grated Cheddar cheese, if desired. Makes 6 to 8 servings.

Variation

Substitute 1-1/2 cups elbow macaroni for tubetti and canned garbanzo or green beans for kidney beans.

Salads

Some of the most versatile salad pastas are elbow macaroni and shells. They can be served in a hot salad such as Hot Spinach Salad, in a cold salad such as Salonika Salad, or in a mold like Molded Macaroni Salad.

Pasta and fruit are an unbelievable natural in Party Chicken Salad and Sea Shell Fruit Salad. Even if combining pasta and fruit is a new idea for you, I'm sure you'll enjoy it. You can toss pasta shells with any fruit salad. Imagine fruit tossed with noodles made from Orange Pasta or Pineapple Pasta! The recipes for flavored pastas are on pages 14 to 20.

Caesar Salad has a new look and taste when fried spicy chips are added to it. I cut the noodles—made from Spicy Italian Pasta, page 15—into small chips. Then I deep-fry them and sprinkle the fried chips on top of the greens. These chips can be made ahead and stored in an airtight container. Use them as a topping for any crisp green salad.

If you are going to use pasta in a cold salad, rinse it in cold water after it has been cooked and drained. This stops the cooking and chills the pasta so it's ready to be tossed with the dressing.

Menu
Patio Picnic
Char-Broiled Steak
Buttered Roasted Corn
Three-Bean Salad, page 47
Molded Macaroni Salad, page 49
Herb-Buttered French Bread
Watermelon
Iced Tea

Lasagne Salad Supreme

Torn salad greens are less likely to be bruised, so the salad will stay fresh longer.

2 qts. water
1 teaspoon salt
2 teaspoons vegetable oil
4 lasagne noodles, uncooked
1/2 cup Italian salad dressing
6 cups torn, assorted salad greens
2 green onions, sliced

6 slices salami, cut in julienne strips
6 oz. brick cheese, cut in strips
1 (14-oz.) can artichoke hearts, drained, quartered
1 cup garlic-flavored croutons
1/4 cup grated Parmesan cheese

Bring water to a rapid boil in a heavy 4-quart saucepan. Add salt and oil. Gradually add lasagne noodles, being sure water continues to boil. Cook noodles uncovered until tender but firm, stirring occasionally. Drain. Rinse with cold water. Drain again. Cut noodles into 1/4" x 2" strips. Place cut noodles in a large salad bowl. Add salad dressing and toss well. Add salad greens, green onions, salami, cheese strips, artichoke hearts, croutons and Parmesan cheese. Toss to coat all ingredients. Serve immediately. Makes 4 to 6 servings.

Antipasto Salad

Make this the first course for your next pasta party.

4 oz. hard salami, diced
1 small red onion, thinly sliced,
   separated into rings
1 cup whole pitted ripe olives
8 oz. fresh mushrooms, sliced
1 (14-oz.) can artichoke hearts,
   drained, quartered
1/2 cup Italian dressing
6 cups water
1 teaspoon salt

1 tablespoon vegetable oil
2 cups large shell macaroni, uncooked (8 oz.)
1 cup diagonally sliced celery
1 cup cherry tomatoes, cut in half
1/2 cup diced green pepper
6 oz. Swiss cheese, cut in thin strips
1 teaspoon salt
1/4 teaspoon black pepper
12 slices hard salami for garnish

In a medium bowl, place salami, onion, olives, mushrooms and artichoke hearts. Add dressing; toss to coat ingredients. Cover and marinate in refrigerator 3 hours. One hour before serving, bring water to a rapid boil in a heavy 4-quart saucepan. Add 1 teaspoon salt and oil. Gradually add macaroni, being sure water continues to boil. Cook macaroni uncovered until tender but firm, stirring occasionally. Drain. Rinse with cold water. Drain again. Place in a large salad bowl. Add celery, tomatoes, green pepper, cheese, 1 teaspoon salt, pepper and marinated vegetables. Toss lightly. Refrigerate 30 minutes. Garnish rim of bowl with salami slices folded in quarters for a ruffled effect. Makes 10 servings.

Macaroni Relish Loaf

Fresh jellied relish loaf goes well with slices of cold roast beef.

3 cups water
1/2 teaspoon salt
1 teaspoon vegetable oil
1/2 cup elbow macaroni, uncooked (2 oz.)
2 pkgs. unflavored gelatin
1 cup cold water
1 cup boiling water
2/3 cup Russian salad dressing
2/3 cup chopped white cabbage
1/4 cup lemon juice

2 tablespoons minced pimiento
2 tablespoons minced green pepper
1 tablespoon grated onion
1 teaspoon salt
1/2 teaspoon Worcestershire sauce
1/8 teaspoon Tabasco sauce
Lettuce leaves
Parsley for garnish
Green pepper strips for garnish

Bring 3 cups water to a rapid boil in a heavy 2-quart saucepan. Add 1/2 teaspoon salt and oil. Gradually add macaroni, being sure water continues to boil. Cook macaroni uncovered until tender but firm, stirring occasionally. Drain. Rinse with cold water. Drain again. Chill. Lightly oil a 9" x 5" loaf pan; set aside. In a medium bowl, soften gelatin in 1 cup cold water, 5 minutes. Add 1 cup boiling water; stir to dissolve gelatin. Refrigerate until slightly thickened. Add salad dressing. Beat with electric mixer on low speed until frothy. Add chilled, cooked macaroni, cabbage, lemon juice, pimiento, green pepper, onion, 1 teaspoon salt, Worcestershire sauce and Tabasco sauce. Pour into prepared pan. Refrigerate until firm, 3 to 4 hours. At the same time, refrigerate a medium platter. To unmold, place chilled platter over relish loaf in pan. Invert pan and platter; remove pan. Arrange lettuce around mold. Garnish relish loaf with parsley and green pepper strips. Makes 8 servings.

Sicilian Vegetable Salad

Italian dressing adds a pleasant, tangy taste.

6 cups water
1 teaspoon salt
1 tablespoon vegetable oil
2 cups elbow macaroni, uncooked (8 oz.)
1/4 cup Italian dressing
1 tablespoon white wine vinegar
1/8 teaspoon Worcestershire sauce
1 cup mayonnaise-style salad dressing

2 cups thinly sliced lettuce
2 cups frozen mixed vegetables,
   cooked, drained
1 cup diced process cheese (4 oz.)
2 tablespoons minced onion
1/2 teaspoon salt
Garlic powder to taste
Black pepper to taste

Bring water to a rapid boil in a heavy 4-quart saucepan. Add 1 teaspoon salt and oil. Gradually add macaroni, being sure water continues to boil. Cook macaroni uncovered until tender but firm, stirring occasionally. Drain. Rinse with cold water. Drain again; set aside. In a small bowl, blend Italian dressing, vinegar, Worcestershire sauce and mayonnaise-style salad dressing with a fork or whisk; set aside. In a large bowl, combine cooked macaroni, lettuce, mixed vegetables, cheese, onion, 1/2 teaspoon salt, garlic powder and pepper. Add salad dressing mixture and toss gently to coat all ingredients. Refrigerate 15 minutes before serving. Makes 6 to 8 servings.

How To Make Macaroni Relish Loaf

1/After beating gelatin mixture until frothy, mix in vegetables, cooked macaroni and seasonings. Pour mixture into prepared pan.

2/After refrigerating macaroni loaf until firm, unmold onto a chilled plate and garnish. Mold may be prepared a day before serving.

Salonika Salad

Greek feta cheese may be available in bulk form or in jars in a cheese or gourmet shop.

Garlic & Oil Dressing, see below
6 cups water
1 teaspoon salt
1 tablespoon vegetable oil
2 cups large shell macaroni, uncooked (8 oz.)
1 small head lettuce, broken into
   bite-size pieces
1/4 small head red cabbage, thinly sliced
2 to 4 endive leaves, thinly sliced

3 green onions, thinly sliced
2 small tomatoes, cut in eighths
1/2 (14-oz.) can artichoke hearts,
   drained, quartered
1/2 cup mild pickled peppers
   (about 1-1/2 inches long)
6 ripe olives
2 oz. feta cheese, crumbled
6 anchovy fillets for garnish

Garlic & Oil Dressing:
1 garlic clove, pressed
2 teaspoons salt
1/8 teaspoon black pepper
1/2 cup olive oil

1/3 cup white wine vinegar
2 tablespoons lemon juice
1 tablespoon dried oregano
1/8 teaspoon dried tarragon

Prepare Garlic & Oil Dressing. Set aside. Bring water to a rapid boil in a heavy 4-quart saucepan. Add salt and oil. Gradually add macaroni, being sure water continues to boil. Cook macaroni until tender but firm, stirring occasionally. Drain. Rinse with cold water. Drain again. Place cooked macaroni in a medium bowl. Toss with 1 tablespoon Garlic & Oil Dressing. Refrigerate while preparing salad greens. In a large salad bowl, combine lettuce, cabbage, endive, green onions, tomatoes, artichoke hearts, peppers and ripe olives. Add chilled, cooked macaroni. Toss with about 1/2 cup Garlic & Oil Dressing or just enough to coat the greens. Sprinkle with feta cheese. Garnish with anchovy fillets. Makes 8 servings.

Garlic & Oil Dressing:
In a medium jar with a tight lid, combine all ingredients. Shake well. Store leftover dressing in the refrigerator. Makes about 1 cup.

When substituting fresh herbs for dry herbs, use 1 teaspoon dried herbs for each tablespoon fresh herbs.

Sea Shell Fruit Salad

Make extra Citrus Fruit Dressing. It's excellent with coleslaw.

1 (1-lb.-4-oz.) can pineapple chunks
Citrus Fruit Dressing, see below
6 cups water
1 teaspoon salt
1 tablespoon vegetable oil
2 cups large shell macaroni, uncooked (8 oz.)

1 (11-oz.) can mandarin oranges, drained
1/2 lb. cooked ham, cut in thin strips
1/2 cup cubed Cheddar or Swiss cheese (2 oz.)
1/2 cup sliced water chestnuts, drained
Lettuce cups

Citrus Fruit Dressing:
1 egg, beaten
3 tablespoons sugar

1/4 cup orange juice
2 tablespoons reserved pineapple juice

Drain pineapple; reserve 2 tablespoons pineapple juice for dressing. Prepare Citrus Fruit Dressing. Bring water to a rapid boil in a heavy 3-quart saucepan. Add salt and oil. Gradually add maca-roni, being sure water continues to boil. Cook macaroni uncovered until tender but firm, stirring occasionally. Drain. Rinse with cold water. Drain again. In a large bowl, gently combine cooked macaroni, drained pineapple chunks, mandarin oranges, ham, cheese and water chestnuts. Add Citrus Fruit Dressing to salad. Toss gently to coat all ingredients. Refrigerate 15 minutes. Serve in lettuce cups. Makes 6 to 8 servings.

Citrus Fruit Dressing:
Combine all ingredients in a 1-quart saucepan. Bring to a boil over medium heat, stirring constantly. Boil 1 minute. Chill.

Variation
Sea Shell Fruit Salad With Yogurt Dressing: Blend 1/3 cup mayonnaise-style salad dressing, 1/3 cup plain yogurt and 1/8 teaspoon salt. Substitute yogurt dressing for Citrus Fruit Dressing.

Make a quick salad with leftover cooked noodles, raw or cooked vegetables and bite-size cubes of cooked meat. Toss your improvised salad with your favorite salad dressing.

Tuna In Tomatoes

Minced vegetables add crunch to this colorful and easy-to-prepare salad.

6 cups water
1 teaspoon salt
1 tablespoon vegetable oil
2 cups shell or elbow macaroni,
   uncooked (8 oz.)
1 (7-oz.) can tuna, drained, flaked
1/2 cup minced celery
1/4 cup chopped sweet pickle
1/4 cup minced green pepper
1/2 cup cubed Swiss cheese

2 tablespoons minced onion
1/2 cup mayonnaise-style salad dressing
1/4 cup plain yogurt
1 teaspoon lemon juice
1/4 teaspoon salt
White pepper to taste
4 medium tomatoes
4 lettuce leaves
Salt to taste
Parsley sprigs for garnish

Bring water to a rapid boil in a heavy 4-quart saucepan. Add 1 teaspoon salt and oil. Gradually add macaroni, being sure water continues to boil. Cook macaroni uncovered until tender but firm, stirring occasionally. Drain. Rinse with cold water. Drain again. Place macaroni in a large salad bowl with tuna, celery, sweet pickle, green pepper, cheese and onion. Set aside. In a small bowl, combine mayonnaise-style salad dressing, yogurt, lemon juice, 1/4 teaspoon salt and pepper. Add to tuna mixture. Toss to coat all ingredients. Chill. Place tomatoes stem-end down on lettuce leaves. Cut each tomato from top center down to about 1/4 inch from the stem end, making 6 equal sections. Spread sections apart. Sprinkle with salt to taste. Fill with chilled tuna salad. Garnish with parsley sprigs. Makes 4 servings.

Party Chicken Salad

Chop the avocado and add it to the salad if you prefer. Then spoon the salad into lettuce cups.

3 cups water
1/2 teaspoon salt
1 teaspoon vegetable oil
1/2 cup small shell or salad macaroni,
   uncooked (2 oz.)
2 cups cubed cooked chicken
1/2 cup pineapple chunks, drained
1/2 cup chopped celery
1/2 cup cooked peas

1 tablespoon capers, drained
1/3 cup white wine vinegar
2 tablespoons sugar
1/2 teaspoon salt
White pepper to taste
2 avocados, halved
2 tablespoons toasted slivered almonds,
   if desired
Lettuce leaves

Bring water to a rapid boil in a heavy 2-quart saucepan. Add 1/2 teaspoon salt and oil. Gradually add macaroni, being sure water continues to boil. Cook macaroni uncovered until tender but firm, stirring occasionally. Drain. Rinse with cold water. Drain again. In a medium bowl, combine cooked macaroni, chicken, pineapple chunks, celery, peas and capers. Set aside. In a small saucepan, heat vinegar and sugar until sugar dissolves. Add 1/2 teaspoon salt and pepper. Cool. Add dressing to salad and toss. Spoon into avocado halves. Sprinkle with almonds. Serve on lettuce-lined salad plates. Makes 4 servings.

Caesar Salad

The fresh egg yolk coats the ingredients and enhances the flavor.

Vinaigrette Dressing, see below
Spicy Italian Pasta dough, page 15
Vegetable oil for deep-frying
1 small head romaine lettuce, torn
   (about 4 cups)

1 small head iceberg or Bibb lettuce, torn
1 egg yolk
2 tablespoons grated Parmesan cheese

Vinaigrette Dressing:
1/2 cup vegetable oil
2-1/2 tablespoons white wine vinegar
3/4 teaspoon salt
1/2 teaspoon sugar

1/8 teaspoon dry mustard
Garlic powder to taste
Freshly ground black pepper to taste

Prepare Vinaigrette Dressing; set aside. Roll 1/4 Spicy Italian Pasta dough by hand or with a pasta machine to a 1/16-inch thick rectangle. Using a pastry cutter, cut into 1" x 3/4" rectangle. Repeat with remaining dough. Heat oil to 365°F (185°C). At this temperature a 1-inch cube of bread will turn golden brown in 50 to 60 seconds. Fry noodle chips in hot oil about 30 seconds, until golden. Drain on paper towels. Set aside 1 cup fried chips for salad. Place Romaine and iceberg or Bibb lettuce in a large salad bowl. Place yolk on top of greens. Pour Vinaigrette Dressing over yolk. Toss to coat greens with yolk and dressing. Sprinkle cheese over salad and toss again. Top with 1 cup fried chips. Serve remaining fried chips as a snack. Makes 6 servings.

Vinaigrette Dressing:
In a small jar with a tight lid, combine all ingredients. Shake well. Store any leftover dressing in the refrigerator. Makes about 1/2 cup.

Tasty Tuna Salad

Subtly flavored dressing takes this tuna salad out of the ordinary.

6 cups water
1 teaspoon salt
1 tablespoon vegetable oil
2 cups large shell macaroni, uncooked (8 oz.)
2 tablespoons lemon juice
2 tablespoons Italian dressing
1/2 cup mayonnaise-style salad dressing

Worcestershire sauce to taste
Salt and black pepper to taste
2 (7-oz.) cans tuna, drained, flaked
1 cup thinly sliced leaf lettuce
1/3 cup thinly sliced celery
1/4 cup pimiento-stuffed olives

Bring water to a rapid boil in a heavy 4-quart saucepan. Add 1 teaspoon salt and oil. Gradually add macaroni, being sure water continues to boil. Cook macaroni uncovered until tender but firm stirring occasionally. Drain; rinse with cold water. Drain again; set aside. In a small bowl, blend lemon juice, Italian dressing, mayonnaise-style salad dressing, Worcestershire sauce and salt and pepper to taste with a fork or whisk. In a large bowl, lightly toss cooked macaroni, tuna, lettuce, celery, olives and salad dressing mixture. Refrigerate 15 minutes before serving. Makes 6 servings.

Hot Spinach Salad

Serve this hot salad with slices of cold beef or ham and cheese bread.

4 cups water
1/2 teaspoon salt
1 teaspoon vegetable oil
1 cup elbow macaroni, uncooked (4 oz.)
6 slices bacon, diced
2 tablespoons chopped onion
2 teaspoons flour
1 tablespoon sugar

1/2 teaspoon salt
1/2 teaspoon dry mustard
1/4 teaspoon black pepper
Garlic powder to taste
1/2 cup water
3 tablespoons white wine vinegar
1 egg
1/2 lb. leaf spinach, torn (about 5 cups)

Bring 4 cups water to a rapid boil in a heavy 2-quart saucepan. Add 1/2 teaspoon salt and oil. Gradually add macaroni, being sure water continues to boil. Cook macaroni uncovered until tender but firm, stirring occasionally. Drain. Rinse with cold water. Drain again; set aside. In a medium skillet, cook bacon until crisp. Drain off fat, reserving 1/4 cup in skillet. Sauté onion in reserved drippings. Stir in flour. Continue stirring over medium heat, about 1 minute. Add sugar, 1/2 teaspoon salt, dry mustard, pepper and garlic powder. Blend 1/2 cup water into flour mixture a little at a time, stirring constantly. Stir in vinegar. Continue to stir over medium heat until thickened. Remove from heat. In a small bowl, beat egg slightly with a fork or whisk. Stir 2 tablespoons hot mixture into beaten egg. Slowly stir egg mixture into hot mixture. In a large salad bowl, mix cooked macaroni, spinach and cooked bacon. Add hot dressing; toss well to coat all ingredients. Serve immediately. Makes 4 to 6 servings.

Three-Bean Salad

Save the bean liquid and use it in your favorite soup.

1 (16-oz.) can wax beans, drained
1 (16-oz.) can diagonal cut green beans, drained
1 (16-oz.) can dark red kidney beans, drained
2/3 cup minced celery
1/3 cup minced green pepper
1/4 cup minced onion
1 (2-oz.) jar pimientos, drained, chopped
2/3 cup white wine vinegar

1/3 cup vegetable oil
1/2 cup sugar
1 teaspoon salt
1 teaspoon black pepper
6 cups water
1 teaspoon salt
1 tablespoon vegetable oil
2 cups large shell macaroni, uncooked (4 oz.)

In a large bowl, combine wax beans, green beans, kidney beans, celery, green pepper, onion and pimientos. Set aside. In a small bowl, blend vinegar, 1/3 cup oil, sugar, 1 teaspoon salt and pepper with a fork or whisk. Pour over bean mixture. Toss to coat evenly. Cover and refrigerate 6 hours or overnight. One hour before serving, bring water to a rapid boil in a heavy 4-quart saucepan. Add 1 teaspoon salt and 1 tablespoon oil. Gradually add macaroni, being sure water continues to boil. Cook macaroni uncovered until tender but firm, stirring occasionally. Drain. Rinse with cold water. Drain again. Fold into bean mixture. Refrigerate until serving time. Makes 8 to 10 servings.

Picnic Salad

Rinsing the pasta with cold water stops the cooking and cools the pasta.

6 cups water
1 teaspoon salt
1 tablespoon vegetable oil
2 cups small shell macaroni, uncooked (8 oz.)
1/2 cup mayonnaise-style salad dressing
2 tablespoons sweet pickle liquid
1 tablespoon Dijon-style mustard
1/2 teaspoon prepared horseradish
1/2 teaspoon salt

White pepper to taste
1/2 cup sliced celery
1/2 cup sliced sweet gherkins
1/3 cup sliced radishes
1 green onion, thinly sliced
1 cucumber, cut in 1/2-inch by
   1-1/2-inch strips
1 carrot, cut in 1/4-inch by
   1-1/2-inch strips

Bring water to a rapid boil in a heavy 4-quart saucepan. Add 1 teaspoon salt and oil. Gradually add macaroni, being sure water continues to boil. Cook macaroni uncovered until tender but firm, stirring occasionally. Drain. Rinse with cold water. Drain again; set aside to cool. In a large salad bowl, stir salad dressing until creamy. Blend in pickle liquid, mustard, horseradish, 1/2 teaspoon salt and pepper. Add cooked macaroni, celery, sweet gherkins, radishes, green onion, cucumber and carrot. Toss to coat all ingredients. Refrigerate until serving time. Makes 4 to 6 servings.

Coleslaw

Brick cheese is a semisoft cheese loaf similar to Muenster and Monterey Jack.

Creamy Coleslaw Dressing, see below
4 cups water
1/2 teaspoon salt
1 teaspoon vegetable oil
1 cup elbow macaroni, uncooked (4 oz.)

3 cups shredded white cabbage
2 oz. brick cheese cut in julienne strips
   (about 1/2 cup)
1/4 cup finely grated carrot
2 tablespoons chopped onion

Creamy Coleslaw Dressing:
1/2 cup dairy sour cream
1/4 cup mayonnaise-style salad dressing
1 teaspoon sugar
1 teaspoon salt

1/8 teaspoon white pepper
1/4 teaspoon dry mustard
1/4 teaspoon celery seeds

Prepare Creamy Coleslaw Dressing; set aside. Bring water to a rapid boil in a heavy 2-quart saucepan. Add salt and oil. Gradually add macaroni, being sure water continues to boil. Cook macaroni uncovered until tender but firm, stirring occasionally. Drain. Rinse with cold water. Drain again. Place in a large salad bowl. Add cabbage, cheese strips, carrot and onion. Add Creamy Coleslaw Dressing. Toss to coat all ingredients. Refrigerate 30 minutes before serving. Makes 6 to 8 servings.

Creamy Coleslaw Dressing:
In a small bowl, stir sour cream and salad dressing with a fork or whisk until combined. Add sugar, salt, pepper, dry mustard and celery seeds. Stir to combine.

Molded Macaroni Salad

Molded salads will hold their shape better if they're served on a chilled platter.

2 tablespoons mayonnaise-style salad dressing
6 cups water
1 teaspoon salt
2 cups large shell or elbow macaroni, uncooked (8 oz.)
3/4 lb. mortadella, olive or pickle loaf luncheon meat, cut in julienne strips (12 to 15 slices)
1 cup cubed Cheddar cheese (4 oz.)
2 green onions, thinly sliced
1 cup chopped celery
1/3 cup drained pickle relish

3 tablespoons chopped pimiento
1/2 cup mayonnaise-style salad dressing
1/2 cup plain yogurt or dairy sour cream
1/4 lb. American or Monterey Jack cheese cut in julienne strips (4 slices)
1/4 lb. mortadella, olive or pickle loaf luncheon meat, cut in julienne strips (4 slices)
1 green pepper cut in rings
Parsley for garnish
2 tomatoes cut in wedges for garnish
Paprika to taste

With a pastry brush, thoroughly brush a 7-cup mold or bowl with 2 tablespoons mayonnaise-style salad dressing; set aside. Bring water to a rapid boil in a heavy 4-quart saucepan. Add salt. Gradually add macaroni, being sure water continues to boil. Cook macaroni uncovered until tender but firm, stirring occasionally. Drain. Rinse with cold water. Drain again. In a large bowl, toss cooked macaroni, 3/4 pound luncheon meat strips, Cheddar cheese cubes, green onions, celery, pickle relish and pimiento; set aside. In a small bowl, blend 1/2 cup salad dressing and yogurt or sour cream. Add to macaroni mixture; toss to coat all ingredients. Press into prepared mold. Cover and refrigerate overnight. Refrigerate a large platter overnight. To unmold, run a metal spatula around sides of mold to loosen salad. Place chilled platter upside down on mold. Invert mold and platter. Remove mold. Arrange American or Monterey Jack cheese strips and 1/4 pound luncheon meat strips inside pepper rings; place around salad. Garnish with parsley and tomato wedges. Sprinkle with paprika. Makes 6 to 8 servings.

Cut cooked lasagne noodles into bite-size pieces and add them to a tossed salad.

Luncheons

If you're looking for something elegant to serve at your next buffet or brunch, try Broccoli Pasta, page 14, and serve it in Broccoli Beauty Rolls or Broccoli-Cheese Cornucopias.

Experiment with homemade pasta squares and lasagne noodles from the supermarket to make unique sandwiches. I did, and the results are Lasagne Burgers, Surprise Chili Dogs and Double Decker Reubens.

You can entertain and at the same time be free to enjoy the party by preparing several batches of Pasta Flatbread, page 17. Bring out assorted cheeses, cold cuts, relishes and condiments and let your guests put together their own sandwiches. To get you started, try Special Sandwich Rolls and some of the variations listed on page 61.

Pizza with Pizzazz is a basic cheese dish made with Italian sausage and vermicelli. This can be made the day before and reheated or it can be frozen. Serve the pizza with a tossed salad and assorted fruits.

Carrot-Cheese Ravioli can also be made ahead and frozen. The ravioli squares are made with Raw Carrot Pasta, page 18, filled with shredded cheese and spinach and served in a pizza sauce.

Menu
Something Special For The Ladies
Spicy Tomato Juice
Broccoli-Cheese Cornucopias, page 52
Cinnamon Muffins
Butter Curls
Sherbet Ring With Strawberries
Café au Lait

Double Decker Reubens

Steam from a little water on the griddle finishes cooking these open face, stacked sandwiches.

1/3 Whole Wheat Pasta dough, page 15
3 tablespoons butter
1/2 cup Thousand Island dressing
1/2 cup sauerkraut, well drained

8 slices corned beef
8 slices Swiss cheese
3 tablespoons water

Roll out Whole Wheat Pasta dough by hand or with a pasta machine to 1/16 inch thick. Cut in four 5-inch squares. Melt butter on electric griddle set at 325°F (165°C) or on a non-electric griddle over medium-low heat. Carefully place pasta squares on griddle. Brown about 1 minute on each side until golden. Leave squares on griddle. Spread each square with 1 tablespoon Thousand Island dressing. Cover each with 2 tablespoons sauerkraut. Arrange 2 slices corned beef over sauerkraut. Drizzle 1 tablespoon Thousand Island dressing over each stack. Top each stack with 2 slices of cheese. Pour 3 tablespoons water directly onto griddle, being careful water does not touch pasta squares. Immediately cover griddle with foil. Heat until cheese melts and sauerkraut is warm, 1 to 2 minutes. Using a spatula, place one stack on top of another to make 1 sandwich. Repeat with other stacks. Serve immediately. Makes 2 sandwiches.

Chinese Pork & Vegetables

Before you begin to stir-fry, have all ingredients ready to add at the proper time.

10 cups water
2 teaspoons salt
1 tablespoon vegetable oil
1 lb. thin egg noodles, uncooked
2 tablespoons vegetable oil
1 lb. lean pork, cut into paper thin strips
1 garlic clove, pressed
1 tablespoon minced fresh ginger root
1/4 cup soy sauce
3 tablespoons sherry wine
1/2 teaspoon sugar

1/2 cup sliced fresh mushrooms
1/2 cup sliced green onion
1 (16-oz.) can Chinese vegetables, drained, or
   1 (10-oz.) pkg. frozen Chinese vegetables,
   thawed
1 (6-oz.) can water chestnuts, drained, sliced
1 cup beef broth
2 teaspoons cornstarch
1 tablespoon water
2 to 3 tablespoons vegetable oil

Bring 10 cups water to a rapid boil in a heavy 5-quart pot or Dutch oven. Add salt and 1 tablespoon oil. Gradually add noodles, being sure water continues to boil. Cook noodles uncovered until tender but firm, stirring occasionally. Drain. Heat 2 tablespoons oil in a wok or large skillet. Add pork, garlic and ginger root. Stir-fry over high heat until meat is browned. Stir in soy sauce, sherry and sugar. Cook and stir 2 to 3 minutes longer. Add mushrooms, green onion, Chinese vegetables, water chestnuts and broth. Cook 2 minutes longer. Mix cornstarch and 1 tablespoon water. Stir mixture into meat and vegetables. Cook 1 minute or until bubbly and slightly thickened. Place meat and vegetables in a serving dish; keep warm. Stir-fry noodles in 2 to 3 tablespoons of oil in clean wok or skillet. Serve with meat and vegetables. Makes 4 servings.

Mexican Stew

Brushing the avocado slices with lemon juice prevents them from turning brown.

2 tablespoons vegetable oil
1-1/2 lbs. beef stew meat, cut in 1-inch cubes
1/2 cup chopped onion
1 garlic clove, pressed
1/4 cup water
1 (16-oz.) can tomatoes, cut up
4 cups beef broth
1-1/2 teaspoons salt

1/2 teaspoon chili powder
8 oz. mostaccioli, uncooked
2 tablespoons canned chopped green chilies
1 cup canned pinto beans, drained
1/4 cup sliced pimiento-stuffed olives
1 avocado for garnish
Lemon juice
Dairy sour cream for garnish

Heat oil in a large heavy pot or Dutch oven. Add meat, onion and garlic. Sauté until meat is browned on all sides. Add water. Cover and simmer 1 hour, adding more water as needed. Add tomatoes, beef broth, salt and chili powder. Bring to a boil. Stir in mostaccioli, green chilies, pinto beans and olives. Bring to a boil again, stirring constantly. Cover and cook 10 minutes. Uncover; cook 5 minutes longer or until pasta is done. Cut avocado in half lengthwise. Remove seed and peel. Slice avocado crosswise. Brush slices with lemon juice. Place stew on a large warm platter. Garnish with a dollop of sour cream and avocado slices. Makes 6 servings.

Polynesian Pork

If there isn't enough pineapple juice, add water or chicken broth.

1 tablespoon vegetable oil
2 lbs. lean pork, cut in 3-inch wide strips or
    beef sirloin strips
1 garlic clove, pressed
1 tablespoon minced fresh ginger root or
    1/4 teaspoon ground ginger
1 cup hot water
1/3 cup soy sauce
2 (1-lb.-4-oz.) cans pineapple chunks
1/3 cup firmly packed brown sugar

3 tablespoons cornstarch
1/3 cup wine vinegar
2 medium onions, thinly sliced
2 green peppers, cut in thin strips
1 (4-oz.) can water chestnuts, drained, sliced
10 cups water
2 teaspoons salt
1 tablespoon vegetable oil
1 lb. fine noodles, uncooked

Heat 1 tablespoon oil in a large skillet. Sauté pork until golden brown, stirring to separate meat strips. Stir in garlic and ginger. In a small bowl, mix 1 cup hot water and soy sauce. Pour over meat. Cover and simmer 1 hour until tender. Drain pineapple, reserving 2-1/2 cups syrup. Mix reserved syrup, brown sugar, cornstarch and vinegar. Add to pork mixture. Cook and stir frequently until thickened. Add pineapple chunks and onions. Reduce heat and simmer 10 minutes. Add green peppers and water chestnuts. Simmer 5 minutes. Bring 10 cups water to a rapid boil in a heavy 5-quart pot or Dutch oven. Add salt and 1 tablespoon oil. Gradually add noodles, being sure water continues to boil. Cook noodles uncovered until tender but firm, stirring occasionally. Drain. Serve pork mixture over hot cooked noodles. Makes 8 servings.

Broccoli-Cheese Cornucopias

Broccoli wrapped in ham and pasta spills out of miniature horns of plenty.

Cheddar Cheese Sauce, page 134
1/3 Plain Pasta dough, page 14
3 qts. water
1 teaspoon salt
1 (10-oz.) pkg. frozen broccoli spears

1/4 cup boiling water
1/2 teaspoon salt
6 slices ham
1/4 cup shredded Cheddar cheese (1 oz.)
Thin orange slices for garnish

Prepare Cheddar Cheese Sauce; set aside. Butter a 13" x 9" baking dish; set aside. Roll Plain Pasta dough by hand or with a pasta machine 1/16 inch thick. Cut in six 6-inch squares. In a heavy 5-quart saucepan or Dutch oven, bring 3 quarts water to a rapid boil. Add 1 teaspoon salt. Drop pasta squares into boiling water; cook 3 minutes. Carefully remove pasta from water with a slotted spoon. Drain on cloth towels. Cook broccoli in 1/4 cup boiling water with 1/2 teaspoon salt, about 4 minutes. Drain. To assemble, place a slice of ham over each pasta square. Lay broccoli spears from corner to corner of each square. Fold 1 free corner over to cover broccoli. Fold opposite corner over to form a cornucopia. Secure with wooden picks. Place in prepared baking dish. Pour Cheddar Cheese Sauce over cornucopias. Sprinkle shredded Cheddar cheese on top. Place baking dish in cold oven. Set temperature control at 350°F (175°C). Bake 15 to 20 minutes. Remove wooden picks before serving and garnish with thin orange slices. Makes 6 servings.

Lasagne Pizza

No need to preheat the oven if you're just heating food through or melting cheese.

Pizza Sauce, see below
5 qts. water
1 tablespoon salt
1 tablespoon vegetable oil
20 lasagne noodles, uncooked

2-1/4 cups shredded mozzarella cheese (9 oz.)
4 oz. thinly sliced pepperoni
1 (8-oz.) can mushrooms, stems and pieces, drained
1/4 cup diced green pepper

Pizza Sauce:
2 tablespoons vegetable oil
1 tablespoon butter
1/2 cup chopped onion
1/4 cup chopped celery
1 garlic clove, pressed
1 (8-oz.) can tomato sauce
1 (6-oz.) can tomato paste
2 tablespoons grated Parmesan cheese

2 teaspoons dried oregano
1 teaspoon dried basil
1/2 teaspoon salt
1/2 teaspoon sugar
1/2 teaspoon Worcestershire sauce
1/4 teaspoon black pepper
1 small bay leaf

Prepare Pizza Sauce; set aside. Bring water to a rapid boil in a heavy 7-quart pot or Dutch oven. Add salt and oil. Gradually add lasagne noodles, being sure water continues to boil. Cook noodles uncovered until tender but firm, stirring occasionally. Drain. Rinse with cold water. Drain again. Butter a 15" x 10" jelly-roll pan or rimmed baking sheet. Arrange 10 cooked lasagne noodles in pan. Sprinkle with 3/4 cup cheese. Cover with remaining 10 noodles. Spread Pizza Sauce evenly over noodles. Place pizza in cold oven. Set temperature control at 350°F (175°C). Bake 10 minutes. Remove from oven. Arrange pepperoni slices, mushroom stems and pieces and green pepper over pizza. Sprinkle with remaining 1-1/2 cups cheese. Return to oven. Bake until cheese melts, about 15 minutes. Makes 1 large pizza.

Pizza Sauce:

In a medium saucepan, heat oil and butter. Sauté onion, celery and garlic until onion is golden. Stir in tomato sauce, tomato paste, Parmesan cheese, oregano, basil, salt, sugar, Worcestershire sauce, pepper and bay leaf. Simmer until thickened, 15 minutes. Remove bay leaf. Use at once or freeze for future use. Makes about 2-1/2 cups.

Lasagne Pizza is pictured on the following pages.

Lasagne Burgers

Wrap a burger patty in a lasagna noodle and top it with Pizza Sauce!

1 lb. ground beef
1/2 teaspoon salt
1/8 teaspoon black pepper
1/2 teaspoon dried oregano
2 tablespoons butter or margarine
2 qts. water
1 teaspoon salt

2 teaspoons vegetable oil
4 lasagne noodles, uncooked
4 slices mozzarella cheese
12 pimiento-stuffed olives, thinly sliced
3/4 cup Pizza Sauce, page 53
4 teaspoons grated Parmesan cheese
Minced parsley for garnish

Form ground beef into 4 patties. Do not pack tightly. Sprinkle with 1/2 teaspoon salt, pepper and oregano. Melt butter or margarine in large skillet. Brown patties on both sides. Set aside. While patties are cooking, bring water to a rapid boil in a heavy 4-quart saucepan. Add 1 teaspoon salt and oil. Gradually add lasagne noodles, being sure water continues to boil. Cook noodles uncovered until tender but firm, stirring occasionally. Drain. Place cooked lasagne noodles on a flat surface. In the center of each lasagne noodle, layer 1 slice mozzarella cheese, 1/4 of the sliced olives and 1 ground beef patty. Fold both ends of lasagne strip over beef patty. Drain fat from skillet. Arrange lasagne patties seam-side down in skillet. Heat pizza sauce in a small saucepan. Spoon 3 tablespoons sauce over each burger. Sprinkle with Parmesan cheese. Cover and cook over low heat until mozzarella cheese melts, about 3 minutes. Sprinkle with minced parsley before serving. Makes 4 servings.

Asparagus-Ham Bake

If you use curly lasagne, the edges of the roll-ups will have a pretty ruffle.

3 qts. water
2 teaspoons salt
1 tablespoon vegetable oil
8 lasagne noodles, uncooked
1 (10-oz.) can condensed cream of celery soup

1 cup milk
1 slice cooked ham, 1/4 inch thick,
    cut in thin strips (10 oz.)
1 (15-oz.) can asparagus spears
1/2 cup shredded Cheddar cheese (2 oz.)

Bring water to a rapid boil in a heavy 6-quart pot or Dutch oven. Add salt and oil. Gradually add lasagne noodles, being sure water continues to boil. Cook noodles uncovered until tender but firm, stirring occasionally. Drain. Rinse with cold water. Drain again; set aside. In a medium saucepan, blend soup and milk over medium heat. Keep warm. Cut lasagne noodles in half crosswise. Place 2 halves together, overlapping edges to form a square. Divide ham strips and asparagus. Place on center of each lasagne square. Carefully roll squares around ham and asparagus. Pour half of hot soup mixture into an 11" x 7" baking dish. Place lasagne rolls in baking dish, seam-side down. Pour remaining soup mixture over rolls. Place in cold oven. Set temperature control at 400°F (205°C). Bake 10 minutes until golden brown. Makes 4 to 6 servings.

Variation

Substitute cooked and drained broccoli for asparagus and Cheddar cheese soup for celery soup.

Surprise Chili Dogs

Next time you prepare lasagne for the freezer, cook extra noodles and make these for supper.

1 (1-lb. 13-oz.) can tomato puree
1/4 cup water
1/4 cup sugar
1/4 cup sweet relish
2 teaspoons prepared mustard
1 teaspoon salt

1/4 teaspoon black pepper
Garlic powder to taste
3 lasagne noodles, cooked, drained
6 frankfurters
3 slices American cheese

Butter an 11" x 7" baking dish; set aside. In a medium saucepan, mix tomato puree, water, sugar, relish, mustard, salt, pepper and garlic powder. Bring to a boil; reduce heat. Simmer 2 minutes. Slice each frankfurter down the middle but not cutting all the way through. Stuff each frankfurter with 1/2 slice cheese cut in thin strips. Cut each lasagne noodle in half lengthwise to make 2 long strips. Wrap each frankfurter with a noodle strip. Place frankfurter in prepared baking dish so that cheese-filling is on top and ends of noodle strip are underneath. Pour tomato sauce mixture over rolls. Place baking dish in oven. Set temperature control at 400°F (205°C). Bake 10 minutes. Serve immediately. Makes 6 Surprise Chili Dogs.

Variation

Substitute 4 ounces thin egg noodles, cooked, for lasagne. Toss cooked noodles with tomato sauce mixture and spoon into prepared baking dish. Top with cut frankfurters and cheese slices. Bake as directed above.

Noodle Omelet

If you use cooked leftover noodles in this omelet, you'll need about 1 cup.

2 cups water
1/2 teaspoon salt
1 teaspoon vegetable oil
1 cup medium noodles, uncooked (2 oz.)
3 eggs
2 tablespoons grated Parmesan cheese

1 tablespoon milk
1/2 teaspoon salt
1 tablespoon butter
Freshly ground black pepper to taste
Parsley sprigs for garnish

Bring water to a rapid boil in a heavy 2-quart saucepan. Add 1/2 teaspoon salt and oil. Gradually add noodles, being sure water continues to boil. Cook noodles uncovered until tender but firm, stirring occasionally. Drain. Beat eggs in a medium bowl. Add cooked noodles, cheese, milk and 1/2 teaspoon salt. Over medium heat, melt butter in an 8-inch omelet pan or skillet. Pour noodle mixture evenly into preheated pan. Cook 3 to 4 minutes. With a spatula, carefully turn omelet over. Cook about 1 minute more. Place on a warm plate. Sprinkle with pepper. Garnish with parsley sprigs. Makes 2 servings.

Variation

Stir in 1/4 cup ham cubes or crisp bacon chips.

Broccoli Beauty Rolls

Broccoli pasta adds unusual color to this basic meatless dish.

1/2 Broccoli Pasta dough, page 14
4 qts. water
4 teaspoons salt
2 (8-oz.) pkgs. cream cheese, softened

2 tablespoons chopped, drained pimiento
1 tablespoon chopped nuts, if desired
1/3 cup butter

Roll out Broccoli Pasta dough by hand or with a pasta machine 1/16 inch thick. Cut in sixteen 6" x 5" rectangles. Let dry 15 minutes. In a heavy 6-quart pot or Dutch oven, bring water to a rapid boil. Add salt. Drop pasta rectangles 1 at a time into boiling water. Cook about 3 minutes. Carefully remove with a slotted spoon. Drain thoroughly on cloth towels. In a small bowl, mix cream cheese, pimiento and nuts, if desired. Carefully spread 2 tablespoons mixture over each pasta rectangle. Roll up jelly-roll fashion. Secure each roll with 2 wooden picks. Melt butter in a large skillet over medium heat. Carefully sauté rolls on each side until golden brown, 1 to 2 minutes. Remove wooden picks. Serve warm. Makes 6 to 8 servings.

Variation

Substitute Raw Carrot Pasta, page 18, for Broccoli Pasta and sliced ham, bologna or thinly sliced beef for cream cheese. Sliced Swiss or American cheese can be used with the meat slices.

How To Make Broccoli Beauty Rolls

1/Spread about 2 tablespoons cream cheese mixture over each cooked and drained broccoli pasta rectangle.

2/Roll each filled rectangle like a jelly roll, securing each roll with two wooden picks.

Pizza With Pizzazz

Would you believe the crust is made with cooked pasta?

2 qts. water
1-1/2 teaspoons salt
1 tablespoon vegetable oil
3 cups vermicelli, uncooked, broken in half, (6 oz.)
1 lb. bulk Italian sausage
1/3 cup chopped onion
1/3 cup chopped green pepper

1/8 teaspoon black pepper
4 eggs
1 teaspoon cornstarch
3/4 cup milk
1 cup plain yogurt or dairy sour cream
1-1/2 cups shredded Swiss cheese (6 oz.)
2 tablespoons dry breadcrumbs

Butter a 10-inch quiche or deep-dish pie plate; set aside. In a heavy 4-quart saucepan, bring water to a rapid boil. Add salt and oil. Gradually add vermicelli, being sure water continues to boil. Cook vermicelli uncovered until tender but firm, stirring occasionally. Drain; set aside. In a large skillet, break sausage into small pieces. Add onion, green pepper and black pepper. Cook until sausage is no longer pink and onions are golden. Drain off fat; set sausage mixture aside. In a large bowl, beat eggs with a fork or whisk until mixed well but not frothy. Dissolve cornstarch in milk. Blend milk mixture and yogurt or sour cream into eggs. Fold in 1 cup cheese and cooked vermicelli. Spoon into prepared pan. Top with meat mixture. Sprinkle with remaining cheese and breadcrumbs. Place pizza in cold oven. Set temperature control at 350°F (175°C). Bake 40 minutes. Serve hot. Makes 6 to 8 servings.

Double Cheese Bake

Serve this perfect buffet dish with or without chili.

6 cups water
1 teaspoon salt
1 tablespoon vegetable oil
2 cups elbow macaroni, uncooked (8 oz.)
3 tablespoons butter
3/4 cup chopped onion
3/4 cup chopped green pepper
4 eggs

2 cups milk
1 cup shredded Cheddar cheese (4 oz.)
1 cup shredded Swiss cheese (4 oz.)
1 large tomato, diced
2 teaspoons salt
1/4 teaspoon black pepper
4 cups or 2 (15-oz.) cans chili with meat and beans, if desired

Bring water to a rapid boil in a heavy 4-quart saucepan. Add 1 teaspoon salt and oil. Gradually add macaroni, being sure water continues to boil. Cook macaroni uncovered until tender but firm, stirring occasionally. Drain; set aside. Butter a 12-inch quiche pan or a 9-inch square baking dish. Melt butter in a small skillet. Sauté onion and green pepper in butter until onion is golden. In a large bowl, beat eggs until mixed well but not frothy. Stir in milk, Cheddar cheese, Swiss cheese, tomato, 2 teaspoons salt, pepper and sautéed onion mixture. Add cooked macaroni. Spoon into prepared pan. Place pan in cold oven. Set temperature control at 350°F (175°C). Bake 1 hour. Heat chili in a medium saucepan. Spoon hot chili onto each portion of Double Cheese Bake as it is served. Makes 6 to 8 servings.

Noodle Frittata

Almost any vegetable and chopped cooked meat can be added to this Italian omelet.

2 cups water	1 green onion, thinly sliced
1/2 teaspoon salt	1 tablespoon chopped green pepper
1 teaspoon vegetable oil	1/3 cup diced, peeled tomato
1 cup thin noodles, uncooked (2 oz.)	1/8 teaspoon salt
4 eggs	Garlic powder to taste
3 tablespoons grated Parmesan or	White pepper to taste
Romano cheese	2 tablespoons butter

Bring water to a rapid boil in a heavy 2-quart saucepan. Add 1/2 teaspoon salt and oil. Gradually add noodles, being sure water continues to boil. Cook noodles uncovered until tender but firm, stirring occasionally. Drain. Beat eggs in a medium bowl. Add cooked noodles, cheese, onion, green pepper, tomato, 1/8 teaspoon salt, garlic powder and white pepper. Melt butter in an 8-inch omelet pan or skillet. Pour noodle mixture evenly into pan. Cook uncovered over medium heat until most of the liquid has evaporated and omelet is golden brown, 3 to 5 minutes. Remove from heat. Place a large dinner plate upside-down over the pan. Invert pan and plate. Remove the pan. Then carefully slide the omelet from the plate back into pan to cook the other side. Cook 2 to 3 minutes longer to brown. Remove from heat. Carefully transfer the browned omelet onto a hot platter. Serve at once. Makes 2 servings.

Variation

Add 1 slice of ham or salami, cut in thin strips, or 2 slices drained, cooked, chopped bacon to mixture before cooking.

Before adding dried herbs to a dish, always crush them in the palms of your hands to release the aroma.

Special Sandwich Rolls

Use your imagination to make your own perfect sandwich using Pasta Flatbread.

4 Pasta Flatbreads, page 17
Dusseldorf mustard to taste
8 thin slices hard salami, cut in strips

4 thin slices Swiss cheese, cut in strips
1/2 small sweet onion, thinly sliced
Shredded lettuce

Spread Pasta Flatbreads with mustard. Divide salami, cheese, onion and lettuce onto half of each flatbread. Roll up jelly-roll fashion. Secure with wooden picks. Makes 4 sandwiches.

Variations

Fancy Foldovers: Place 2 tablespoons coleslaw and 3 very thin slices cooked ham on half of 1 Pasta Flatbread. Fold other half over to make a sandwich.

Flatbread Tacos: Brown 1/2 pound hamburger. Add 1/2 package taco seasoning and 2 tablespoons water. Simmer 10 minutes over medium heat. Spoon 2 tablespoons meat mixture onto half of 1 Pasta Flatbread. Top with grated cheese, chopped tomato and chopped lettuce. Fold other half of flatbread over. Repeat for additional tacos.

Make-Your-Own Sandwiches: Have ready Pasta Flatbread, sliced cucumbers, sliced tomatoes, thin onion slices, variety of sliced meats, sliced lettuce, mustard, salad dressing or mayonnaise, salt and pepper. The guests put their own sandwiches together on the folded flatbread.

Flatbread Italiano: Cook 4 Italian sausages. In 2 tablespoons vegetable oil, sauté 1 sliced large green pepper and 1 sliced small onion. Place 1 sausage on half of 1 Pasta Flatbread. Top with 1/4 of the sautéed pepper and onion. Fold other half over to form a sandwich. Repeat for additional sandwiches.

Flatbread English Style: Place 2 thin slices roast beef, shredded lettuce, thin tomato slices and creamy horseradish on half of 1 Pasta Flatbread. Fold other half over to make a sandwich.

Pasta should not be stored in the refrigerator in a sauce. The pasta will absorb the sauce and become soft.

Spaghetti With Meatballs

This is a favorite at my house.

2 tablespoons olive oil
1/2 cup chopped onion
2 garlic cloves, pressed
2 (15-oz.) cans tomato sauce
1 (15-oz.) can tomato puree
1 cup water
2 tablespoons minced fresh parsley
1 teaspoon salt
1 tablespoon dried oregano
2 teaspoons Italian herbs

1 teaspoon dried basil
1 teaspoon dried marjoram
1 bay leaf
1/4 teaspoon black pepper
Meatballs, see below
4 qts. water
1 tablespoon salt
1 tablespoon vegetable oil
1 lb. spaghetti, uncooked
Grated Parmesan cheese

Meatballs:
1 lb. ground beef
1/2 lb. ground pork
2 eggs, slightly beaten
1/2 cup fine breadcrumbs
1/4 cup minced fresh parsley
1/4 cup grated Parmesan cheese
3 tablespoons white wine
1 garlic clove, pressed

1 teaspoon salt
1/4 teaspoon black pepper
1/4 teaspoon dried oregano
1/8 teaspoon dried basil
1/8 teaspoon baking soda
2 tablespoons butter
2 tablespoons vegetable oil

In a large heavy pot, heat olive oil. Sauté onion and garlic until onion is golden. Add tomato sauce, tomato puree, 1 cup water, parsley, 1 teaspoon salt, oregano, Italian herbs, basil, marjoram, bay leaf and pepper. Bring to a boil and reduce heat. Cover and simmer 45 minutes. Prepare Meatballs; add to sauce. Cover and simmer 20 minutes longer. Bring 3 quarts water to a rapid boil in a heavy 5-quart pot or Dutch oven. Add 1 tablespoon salt and vegetable oil. Gradually add spaghetti, being sure water continues to boil. Cook spaghetti uncovered until tender but firm, stirring occasionally. Drain. Serve with hot meatball sauce. Top with grated Parmesan cheese. Makes 8 servings.

Meatballs:
In a large bowl, mix ground beef, ground pork, eggs, breadcrumbs, parsley, Parmesan cheese, wine, garlic, salt, pepper, oregano, basil and baking soda. Shape into 24 meatballs. Heat butter and oil in a large skillet. Fry meatballs over low heat, turning to brown on all sides, about 20 minutes.

Martha's Pastitsio

For your next party, try this layered dish from Greece.

1-1/2 lbs. ground beef
1 cup chopped onion
1/4 cup tomato paste
1/3 cup water
1/4 cup dry red wine
1 teaspoon salt
1/4 teaspoon black pepper
1/4 teaspoon cinnamon
2 qts. water

1-1/2 teaspoons salt
1 tablespoon vegetable oil
3/4 lb. mostaccioli, uncooked
3 tablespoons butter, melted
1 egg, beaten
1/4 cup half-and-half
8 oz. grated Parmesan cheese
Creamy Sauce, see below

Creamy Sauce:
1/4 cup butter
1 qt. milk
4 tablespoons cornstarch

Salt to taste
5 eggs

Preheat oven to 350°F (175°C). Butter a 13" x 9" baking dish; set aside. In a large skillet, brown meat and onion, stirring often to break up meat. Add tomato paste, 1/3 cup water, wine, 1 teaspoon salt, pepper and cinnamon. Simmer 10 minutes until liquid evaporates. Bring 2 quarts water to a rapid boil in a heavy 5-quart pot or Dutch oven. Add 1-1/2 teaspoons salt and oil. Gradually add mostaccioli, being sure water continues to boil. Cook mostaccioli uncovered until tender but firm, stirring occasionally. Drain. Pour melted butter over mostaccioli; toss together. In a small bowl, stir egg and half-and-half to blend. Set aside 3 tablespoons Parmesan cheese for topping. Toss egg mixture and remaining cheese with mostaccioli. Place in prepared baking dish. Spread meat sauce over mostaccioli. Pour Creamy Sauce over meat sauce. Sprinkle with remaining 3 tablespoons cheese. Bake in preheated oven 45 minutes until golden. Makes about 6 servings.

Creamy Sauce:
In a medium saucepan, combine butter, milk and cornstarch. Stir over low heat until thickened, about 15 minutes. Stir in salt. Remove from heat. Beat eggs well. Slowly stir about 1 cup hot sauce into beaten eggs. Gradually add egg mixture to sauce; stir to blend. Makes about 5 cups.

Curried Lamb In Noodle Ring

The Noodle Ring is part of the recipe for Glazed Ham Balls In Noodle Ring, page 73.

Noodle Ring, page 73
1/2 cup butter
1 cup thinly sliced green onion
1-1/2 cups diced celery
1/3 cup all-purpose flour
2 cups milk
2 cups chicken broth

1 cup green pepper strips
2 teaspoons curry powder
1/8 teaspoon ground ginger
1/4 teaspoon salt
Freshly ground black pepper to taste
4 cups cubed cooked lamb
Curry Condiments, see below

Curry Condiments:
1/2 cup chopped nuts or peanuts
1/2 cup shredded coconut
3 hard-cooked eggs, chopped

1/2 cup currants, soaked in sherry
1/2 cup chutney

Prepare Noodle Ring. Melt butter in a 2-quart saucepan. Add onion and celery. Sauté until onion is golden. Stir in flour; cook until bubbly. Add milk and chicken broth. Stir constantly over medium heat until thickened. Stir in green pepper, curry powder, ginger, salt and pepper. Add lamb and heat through. Spoon into center of Noodle Ring. Serve with Curry Condiments. Makes 6 to 8 servings.

Curry Condiments:
Place each condiment in its own serving dish.

Variation
Substitute 4 cups cubed cooked chicken or turkey for the lamb.

Leftover cooked noodles are delicious in scrambled eggs and omelets. Use 1/2 cup cooked noodles for each egg.

How To Make
Manicotti With Cheese

1/Slightly undercook manicotti tubes and drain well. Fill with spinach cheese mixture, being careful not to tear the manicotti tubes.

2/If using homemade manicotti sheets, spread about 1/4 cup filling along 1 side and roll up like a jelly roll.

3/Spread 1/3 cup of the Cheese Sauce over bottom of baking dish. Place filled manicotti in dish and spoon about 3 tablespoons sauce over each before baking.

Manicotti With Cheese

The secret to a perfect sauce is to stir constantly until it thickens.

1 (10-oz.) pkg. frozen chopped spinach
Water
Cheese Sauce, see below
2 tablespoons vegetable oil
2 green onions, thinly sliced
2 eggs
1/2 lb. ricotta cheese (1 cup)
1/2 lb. small curd cottage cheese (1 cup)

1/3 cup grated Parmesan cheese
1/2 teaspoon salt
White pepper to taste
10 manicotti tubes, cooked or
    Manicotti, page 20
Paprika for garnish
Fresh mint leaves for garnish

Cheese Sauce:
1/4 cup butter
3 tablespoons flour
3 cups milk

1/2 teaspoon salt
White pepper to taste
1/3 cup grated Parmesan cheese

Cook spinach in water following package directions. Drain well. Prepare Cheese Sauce. In a large skillet heat oil. Sauté onions until golden. In a medium bowl, beat eggs until mixed well but not frothy. Stir in ricotta, cottage cheese, Parmesan cheese, salt and pepper. Add cooked spinach and sautéed onions to cheese mixture; mix well. Stuff manicotti tubes or place about 1/4 cup filling on one side of each cooked manicotti. Roll up like a jelly roll. Spread 1/3 cup Cheese Sauce evenly over bottom of a shallow 13" x 9" baking dish. Place filled manicotti seam-side down in prepared dish. Spoon about 3 tablespoons sauce over each filled manicotti. Place baking dish in cold oven. Set temperature control at 350°F (175°C). Bake 20 minutes. Sprinkle with paprika and garnish with mint leaves. Serve immediately. Makes 12 manicotti.

Cheese Sauce:
In 2-quart saucepan, melt butter over medium heat. Stir in flour. Continue stirring until bubbly. Gradually blend in milk. Stir constantly over medium heat until slightly thickened. Remove from heat. Stir in salt, pepper and cheese. Makes about 3 cups.

Use a long-handled iced-tea spoon to fill manicotti tubes.

Pierogi

Both creamed cottage cheese and dry cottage cheese are used in this Polish favorite.

1 egg
1 cup water
1 tablespoon vegetable oil
1 teaspoon salt
3 cups all-purpose flour

Cottage Cheese Filling, see below
3 qts. water
1 tablespoon salt
Onion Topping, see below

Cottage Cheese Filling:
1 cup dry cottage cheese
1 cup creamed cottage cheese, drained
1 egg, slightly beaten

2 tablespoons instant farina or
   instant cream of wheat

Onion Topping:
1 cup chopped onion
6 tablespoons butter

In a large bowl, beat egg, 1 cup water, oil and 1 teaspoon salt. Stir in flour to make a stiff dough. Let dough rest 5 minutes. Knead until smooth about 10 minutes. Brush top lightly with oil. Cover and let stand 1 hour. Prepare Cottage Cheese Filling. On a lightly floured surface, roll out dough 1/8 inch thick. Use a round cutter to cut into 3-inch circles. With your hands, stretch each circle slightly. Place about 1 heaping teaspoon Cottage Cheese Filling on one side of circle. Fold dough, making a half circle. Seal edges by pressing with a fork. Let Pierogi stand 15 minutes before cooking. In a heavy 5-quart pot or Dutch oven, bring 3 quarts water and 1 tablespoon salt to a boil. Add about 15 Pierogi. Bring to a boil again. Cook 8 to 10 minutes. Drain on paper towels. Place on a platter; keep warm. Repeat until all Pierogi are cooked. Prepare Onion Topping. Serve Pierogi with Onion Topping. Makes 6 to 8 servings.

Cottage Cheese Filling:
In a small bowl, mix together cottage cheeses, egg and farina or cream of wheat.

Onion Topping:
In a small skillet, sauté onion in butter until golden. Keep warm.

Variation
Add 1 teaspoon salt, 1/4 teaspoon white pepper, 2 tablespoons minced fresh parsley, 1 tablespoon snipped chives and 1/8 teaspoon garlic powder to Cottage Cheese Filling. Substitute 1/2 cup butter for the Onion Topping. Melt butter in a heavy skillet until bubbly and golden brown. Pour over hot cooked Pierogi.

Sausage Lasagne

To be sure the egg doesn't separate from the cheeses, bake this in a preheated oven.

3 qts. water
2 teaspoons salt
1 tablespoon vegetable oil
12 strips white or green lasagne noodles
Sausage Sauce, see below.
2 eggs

1 (1-lb.) carton ricotta cheese
1 (1-lb.) carton cottage cheese
1/2 cup grated Parmesan cheese
1/4 teaspoon black pepper
1 lb. thinly sliced mozzarella cheese

Sausage Sauce:
1-1/2 lbs. bulk Italian sausage
1/2 cup chopped mixed carrots, onions, celery
1 (1-lb.) can tomato bits
1 (12-oz.) can tomato paste
1 tablespoon dried parsley flakes
1 garlic clove, pressed

1/2 teaspoon dried oregano
1/4 teaspoon dried basil
1/2 teaspoon salt
1/2 teaspoon sugar
Freshly ground black pepper to taste

Butter a 13" x 9" baking dish; set aside. Bring water to a rapid boil in a heavy 5-quart pot or Dutch oven. Add salt and oil. Gradually add lasagne noodles, being sure water continues to boil. Cook noodles uncovered until tender but firm, stirring occasionally. Drain. Prepare Sausage Sauce; set aside. Preheat oven to 375°F (190°C). Beat eggs in a medium bowl. Stir in ricotta cheese, cottage cheese, Parmesan cheese and pepper; mix well. Spoon 1/2 cup sauce mixture in bottom of prepared baking dish. Place a layer of 6 cooked lasagne noodles over sauce mixture. Spread with half the cheese mixture. Cover with half the mozzarella cheese slices. Spread half the remaining sauce mixture over the cheese. Repeat with remaining 6 lasagne noodles, remaining cheese mixture and remaining sauce mixture. Bake in preheated oven 20 minutes. Remove lasagne from oven. Top with remaining mozzarella cheese slices. Bake 10 minutes longer. Let stand 10 minutes before cutting. Makes 6 to 8 servings.

Sausage Sauce:
In a large skillet, brown sausage about 15 minutes, stirring to break up meat. Drain off excess fat. Stir in remaining ingredients. Cover and simmer 20 minutes or until slightly thickened. Stir occasionally. Makes about 3 cups.

How To Make
Carrot-Cheese Ravioli

1/Place 1 large pasta sheet over ravioli tray, leaving pasta edges extended. Press pasta into tray indentations and fill each indentation with a rounded teaspoon of spinach-cheese mixture.

2/Carefully place a large pasta sheet over spinach-cheese mixture; pasta edges will extend over edge of tray.

3/Using a rolling pin, firmly roll in both directions over fluted edges of each ravioli until all have been cut and sealed. Turn tray upside-down to remove ravioli.

Carrot-Cheese Ravioli

Uncooked ravioli freezes well, so you can double the filling and use all the pasta.

1 (10-oz.) pkg. frozen chopped spinach, cooked, drained
1 cup shredded Cheddar cheese (4 oz.)
1/2 Raw Carrot Pasta dough, page 18
3 cups water

1 (15-oz.) can pizza sauce or 2 cups Classic Tomato Sauce, page 138
1 teaspoon oregano
Grated Romano cheese for garnish

Squeeze spinach to remove excess water. Mix spinach and cheese in a small bowl; set aside. Divide pasta dough into 4 equal balls. By hand or with a pasta machine, roll 2 balls of dough into two 13" x 5" rectangles, 1/8-inch thick. On 1 of the rectangles, place spinach filling by rounded teaspoonfuls in 2 rows of 6 mounds each. Mounds should be about 2 inches apart. Cover with the second pasta rectangle. Use your fingers to press around each mound of filling. With a pastry cutter, cut between the mounds to make 12 ravioli. If using a knife to cut between the squares, press with a fork to seal edges after cutting. Repeat with remaining 2 balls of dough. **If using a ravioli form**, place 1 pasta rectangle over the indented tray. Place plastic insert onto dough to make indentations. Remove insert. Place about 1 rounded teaspoon filling into each indentation. Place another pasta rectangle over the top. With a rolling pin, roll firmly back and forth over flutted edges on the indented tray to trim off excess dough and cut into ravioli squares. Remove individual ravioli from tray, checking edges for poor seal. Repeat with remaining 2 rolls of pasta dough. Place cut ravioli on a lightly floured cloth towel to dry before cooking, about 1 hour. In a large pot or Dutch oven, combine water, pizza sauce or Classic Tomato Sauce and oregano. Bring to a boil. Add ravioli a few at a time, being sure sauce mixture continues to boil. Cook until edges are tender, about 5 minutes. Remove from sauce with a slotted spoon. Pour sauce over ravioli to serve. Have grated Romano cheese available to sprinkle over individual servings. Uncooked ravioli may be frozen. To cook frozen ravioli, drop directly into the boiling liquid; cook until edges are tender, about 8 minutes. Makes 24 ravioli, about 4 servings.

Meat & Poultry

Be unconventional and replace traditional oven-baked potatoes with pasta when making a roast. Try Spaghetti Roast au Jus. In this recipe, spaghetti is baked in the seasoned beef juices. For company, serve Sunday Roast Supreme, or any beef roast, with nutritious Whole-Wheat Pasta, page 15. Ever-popular chuck roast is really special when it's served with hot noodles in Onion Chuck Roast.

Any pasta and poultry combination is high in protein and a nutritious budget-stretcher. Country Chicken and Chicken-In-A-Pan are examples. Whenever I find a sale on chickens, I always buy several and freeze them with these recipes in mind.

If you're looking for a main dish to make in a hurry, Quick Chili Beef takes less than 30 minutes to prepare.

And finally, I couldn't resist the temptation to cook pasta in beer. The result is Milwaukee-Style Beef & Beer—robust and tasty cubes of beef served over hot noodles.

Of course, you'll drink whatever wine your taste and budget dictate. But if you're confused about wines, here are some simple guidelines: Robust main dishes with red meat and red sauces go well with dry or semi-dry red wines. Serve red wines at room temperature. Delicate white meat or seafood and fish go well with a white wine which should be served chilled.

Menu
Favorite Famiy Dinner
Quick Vermicelli Soup, page 34
Beef Stew Mostaccioli, page 78
Leafy Green Salad Bowl With Red Cabbage
Popovers
Raspberry Sherbet

Orange-Ginger Ham

Orange sauce with mustard and wine gives a pleasant taste.

1/4 cup frozen orange juice concentrate,
   thawed
1/4 cup dry white wine
1 teaspoon dry mustard
1/4 teaspoon dried ground ginger

1 (2-lb.) fully cooked ham slice, 1-inch thick
6 canned peach halves
Butter
Orange Pasta dough, page 14,
   cut in noodles, cooked, drained

In a small bowl, combine orange juice concentrate, wine, mustard and ginger. Slash fat at 1-inch intervals to prevent ham from curling. Brush orange sauce over ham. Broil 3 inches from heat, about 10 minutes. Turn. Brush ham with orange sauce. Continue broiling until golden, about 6 minutes. During last 5 minutes of cooking, brush peach halves with orange sauce. Broil with ham. Serve with hot buttered noodles. Makes 6 servings.

Glazed Ham Balls In Noodle Ring

Don't use oil when you cook the noodles. You want them to cling together.

1/2 lb. ground ham
3/4 lb. lean ground pork
2/3 cup quick-cooking oats, uncooked
1 egg, slightly beaten

1/2 cup milk
Fruit Sauce, see below
Noodle Ring, see below

Noodle Ring:

6 cups water
1 teaspoon salt
4 cups medium noodles, uncooked (8 oz.)
2 eggs

2 cups milk
3/4 teaspoon salt
2 tablespoons butter
1/2 cup soft breadcrumbs

Fruit Sauce:

6 whole cloves
1/3 cup firmly packed brown sugar
2 tablespoons all-purpose flour
1 teaspoon dry mustard

1-1/2 cups fruit juice (pineapple or apricot)
2 tablespoons vinegar
1/3 cup light corn syrup

Combine ham, pork, oats, egg and milk in a medium bowl. Mix thoroughly. Cover and refrigerate 30 minutes. Prepare Fruit Sauce and set aside. Shape meat mixture into 1-inch balls and place in an 11" x 7" shallow baking dish. Place in cold oven. Set temperature control at 325°F (165°C). Bake 1 hour. While ham balls are baking, prepare Noodle Ring. Drain excess fat from ham balls. Pour Fruit Sauce over ham balls in baking dish. Bake 15 minutes longer. Fill center of unmolded Noodle Ring with hot ham balls and Fruit Sauce. Makes 6 to 8 servings.

Noodle Ring:
Bring water to a rapid boil in a heavy 3-quart saucepan. Add 1 teaspoon salt. Gradually add noodles, being sure water continues to boil. Cook noodles uncovered until tender but firm, stirring occasionally. Drain. Do not rinse. Preheat oven to 325°F (165°C). Generously butter a 1-1/2-quart ring mold. Place noodles in ring mold. In a medium bowl, beat eggs. Stir in milk and 3/4 teaspoon salt. Pour egg mixture over noodles. Melt butter in a small saucepan or skillet. Add breadcrumbs. Toss lightly to coat. Sprinkle buttered breadcrumbs over egg mixture. Bake in preheated oven 45 minutes. Let Noodle Ring stand 8 to 10 minutes before unmolding. Carefully loosen edges of ring with a metal spatula. Unmold onto warm platter.

Fruit Sauce:
Tie cloves in a piece of cheesecloth. In a 1-quart saucepan, combine brown sugar, flour, mustard, fruit juice, vinegar, corn syrup and bag of cloves. Stirring constantly, cook over medium heat until slightly thickened. Remove bag of cloves. Makes about 2 cups.

Meat-Stuffed Eggplant

Risino—tiny rice—is traditionally used in soup.

2 medium eggplants
1 lb. ground lamb or beef
2 medium onions, thinly sliced
1/2 cup chopped celery with tops
1/2 cup risino macaroni, uncooked
5 parsley sprigs, minced

1 garlic clove, minced
1 teaspoon salt
Black pepper to taste
1 (15-oz.) can herbed tomato sauce
1/2 cup crumbled blue cheese or feta cheese

Butter a shallow 13" x 7" baking dish; set aside. Cut eggplants in half lengthwise; scoop out pulp from center and chop. In a large saucepan or skillet, combine meat, pulp, onions, celery, risino, parsley and garlic. Cook until meat is browned, about 10 minutes, stirring to break up meat. Add salt and pepper. Stir in tomato sauce. Cover and cook to reduce sauce slightly, about 10 minutes. Spoon meat mixture into eggplant shells. Arrange in prepared baking dish. Sprinkle with cheese. Place baking dish in cold oven. Set temperature control at 400°F (205°C). Bake 25 minutes. Cut in half to serve, if desired. Makes 4 to 6 servings.

Upside-Down Ham Loaf

Surprise! It looks like an upside-down cake.

2 eggs
3/4 cup milk
1-1/2 tablespoons prepared mustard
1/8 teaspoon ground cloves
1-1/4 lbs. ground cooked ham
3/4 lb. lean ground pork
1 cup fine cracker crumbs
3 tablespoons brown sugar

6 pineapple slices
6 maraschino cherries
2 qts. water
1 tablespoon vegetable oil
Pineapple Pasta dough, page 14,
    cut in noodles, uncooked
2 tablespoons butter, melted
Parsley sprigs for garnish

Generously grease bottom and sides of a heavy 10-inch skillet; set aside. In a large bowl, beat eggs slightly. Add milk, mustard and cloves. Blend. Add ham, pork and cracker crumbs; mix thoroughly; set aside. Melt brown sugar in prepared skillet. Arrange pineapple slices over sugar. Place a cherry in center of each pineapple slice. Carefully pat meat mixture over pineapple slices. If you have a thermostatically controlled burner, set it at 250°F (120°C), otherwise use medium-low heat. Cover skillet and cook about 5 minutes. Reset control at 200°F (95°C) or reduce heat to low. Cook 1 hour. Fifteen minutes before ham loaf is done, bring water to a rapid boil in a heavy 4-quart saucepan. Add oil. Gradually add noodles, being sure water continues to boil. Cook noodles uncovered until tender but firm, about 5 minutes, stirring occasionally. Drain and coat with butter. Drain excess fat from ham loaf. Place a large round platter upside-down over skillet. Using pot holders, invert skillet and platter. Remove skillet. Arrange buttered noodles around ham loaf. Serve immediately. Garnish with parsley sprigs. Makes 6 to 8 servings.

Variation

Use a medium tube pan and bake in a 325°F (165°C) oven 1 hour.

Spaghetti Roast au Jus

Baking at this low temperature makes a more tender, jucier and better-flavored roast.

1-1/2 teaspoons salt
1 teaspoon beau monde seasoning
1/4 teaspoon black pepper
1/4 teaspoon celery salt

1 (2-1/2- to 3-lb.) beef sirloin tip roast
3-1/2 cups water
8 oz. thin spaghetti, broken in half

In a small bowl, mix salt, beau monde seasoning, pepper and celery salt. Rub on roast. Place roast on rack in a small heavy roasting pan. Add 1/2 cup water. Place roasting pan in cold oven. Set temperature control at 325°F (165°C). Roast 25 to 40 minutes per pound depending on desired doneness. Internal thermometer will read 150° to 170°F (65° to 75°C). Remove roast and pan from oven and place on surface unit of stove. Increase oven temperature to 450°F (230°C). Remove meat from pan; keep warm. Add remaining 3 cups of water to juices in roasting pan. Bring to a boil over medium-high heat. Stir in spaghetti. Bring to a boil again. Cook 4 to 5 minutes, stirring occasionally. Return roasting pan to oven and bake spaghetti about 15 minutes. Place in warm serving dish or platter. Serve with roast beef slices. Makes 4 to 5 servings.

How To Make Upside-Down Ham Loaf

1/Grease bottom and sides of skillet before melting brown sugar. Place a cherry in the center of each pineapple slice. Spoon meat mixture over pineapple slices, patting to make it smooth and even.

2/As ham loaf finishes baking, cook pineapple noodles. Drain excess fat from ham loaf before inverting it onto a warm platter. Spoon cooked noodles around ham loaf.

Onion Chuck Roast

Onion soup mix adds rich flavor to the sauce.

1 (2- to 3-lb.) chuck roast
1 (1-1/4-oz.) pkg. onion soup mix
2 cups water
1 tablespoon butter
1 tablespoon all-purpose flour

2 qts. water
1-1/2 teaspoons salt
1 tablespoon vegetable oil
6 cups thin noodles, uncooked (12 oz.)
Crumbled blue cheese or feta cheese

Place roast in a baking dish and sprinkle with onion soup mix. Pour 1 cup water over all. Cover. Place baking dish in cold oven. Set temperature control at 350°F (175°C). Bake 1 hour. Turn roast and bake 1 hour longer until tender. Remove meat and keep warm. In a small sauce pan, bring remaining 1 cup water to a boil. Pour into drippings. In the same saucepan, melt butter over medium-low heat. Stir in flour. Cook until bubbly, stirring constantly. Gradually blend 1/2 cup drippings mixture into butter mixture. Stir butter mixture into drippings mixture. Stir constantly over medium heat until gravy is slightly thickened. Keep warm. Bring 2 quarts water to a rapid boil in a heavy 4-quart saucepan. Add salt and oil. Gradually add noodles, being sure water continues to boil. Cook noodles uncovered until tender but firm, stirring occasionally. Drain. Place noodles in a large serving dish. Pour gravy over cooked noodles. Sprinkle with crumbled cheese. Serve with roast. Makes 6 to 8 servings.

Festive Tenderloin Tips

To save energy, cook this easy-to-prepare meat dish in your wok.

1-1/2 lbs. beef tenderloin
6 tablespoons butter
1/2 teaspoon salt
1 cup chopped onion
1 cup chopped green pepper
2 cups beef broth
1 tablespoon plus 1 teaspoon cornstarch

1 cup Burgundy wine
1/4 teaspoon salt
Black pepper to taste
6 cups water
1 teaspoon salt
2 teaspoons vegetable oil
4 cups wide noodles, uncooked (8 oz.)

Put meat in freezer for 1 hour. Remove from freezer and slice into 3-inch strips. Melt butter in a large skillet. Sprinkle beef strips with 1/2 teaspoon salt. Brown both sides of strips in butter. Remove from skillet; set aside. Add onion and green pepper to drippings. Sauté until onion is golden, about 3 minutes. Stir in broth. Cook 3 minutes. Dissolve cornstarch in wine. Slowly add to broth mixture, stirring constantly. Add 1/4 teaspoon salt and pepper. Cook and stir until mixture bubbles. Cook 3 minutes longer. Add cooked meat and heat thoroughly. Bring water to a rapid boil in a heavy 3-quart saucepan. Add 1 teaspoon salt and oil. Gradually add noodles, being sure water continues to boil. Cook noodles uncovered until tender but firm, stirring occasionally. Drain. Place in a large serving dish. Pour hot meat mixture over hot noodles. Serve immediately. Makes 6 servings.

Veal Cacciatore

Cacciatore *means* hunter's style *or simmered in an herb, wine and tomato mixture.*

2 lbs. veal steaks, 1/4-inch thick,
  cut in serving pieces
1 teaspoon salt
1/8 teaspoon black pepper
1/4 cup olive oil
1/2 cup chopped onion
1 garlic clove, pressed
1/2 lb. mushrooms, sliced
1 small green pepper, chopped
1/2 cup sliced pimiento-stuffed olives
1 (8-oz.) can tomato sauce

1 cup chicken broth
1/2 cup dry white wine
1/4 teaspoon dried basil
1/4 teaspoon dried mint
1/4 teaspoon dried oregano
6 cups water
1 teaspoon salt
2 teaspoons vegetable oil
4 cups wide noodles, uncooked (8 oz.)
1 tablespoon soft butter
Grated Parmesan cheese

Pound veal into very thin pieces. Sprinkle with salt and pepper. Heat olive oil in a large skillet. Brown veal slowly on all sides. Remove veal from skillet. Sauté onion, garlic, mushrooms and green pepper in drippings until onion is golden. Place in an 11" x 7" baking dish. Sprinkle olives over onion mixture. Arrange veal pieces over olives. Combine tomato sauce, chicken broth, wine, basil, mint and oregano in skillet. Heat and pour over veal. Place baking dish in cold oven. Set temperature control at 350°F (175°C). Bake 30 minutes until tender. Bring water to a rapid boil in a heavy 3-quart saucepan. Add 1 teaspoon salt and vegetable oil. Gradually add noodles, being sure water continues to boil. Cook noodles uncovered until tender but firm, stirring occasionally. Drain. Toss cooked noodles with butter. Serve veal and sauce over hot buttered noodles. Sprinkle with grated Parmesan cheese. Makes 4 servings.

Variation

Substitute a 2-1/2 pound broiler fryer, cut up or a 2 pound sirloin tip roast, sliced thin, for the veal and 2-1/2 cups Classic Tomato Sauce, page 138, for the tomato sauce, broth and wine.

Improvise your own garlic press with two equal-size spoons. Place the garlic clove in the bowl of one spoon, fit the bottom of the other spoon on top of the garlic, and press.

Sunday Roast Supreme

Try this with Whole-Wheat Pasta noodles, page 15.

Beef Roast Marinade, see below
1 (6-lb.) rump roast, rolled, tied
Spinach Pasta dough, page 15,
   cut in noodles, cooked, drained

Butter
Grated Parmesan cheese
Salt and pepper to taste

Beef Roast Marinade:
2-3/4 cups cider vinegar
2-1/3 cups water
3 medium onions, sliced
1 lemon, sliced

1 garlic clove, pressed
2 bay leaves
8 whole cloves
8 whole black peppercorns

Prepare Beef Roast Marinade. Pour over rump roast. Refrigerate 24 to 48 hours, turning meat occasionally. Remove from refrigerator. Insert bulb of meat thermometer as close to center of roast as possible. Place in cold oven. Set temperature control at 325°F (165°C). Bake 25 to 40 minutes per pound depending on desired doneness. Thermometer will read 150° to 170°F (65° to 75°C). During baking, brush occasionally with Beef Roast Marinade. Serve spinach noodles tossed with butter and sprinkled with grated Parmesan cheese. Salt and pepper roast to taste. Makes about 10 servings.

Beef Roast Marinade:
In a medium bowl, combine all ingredients.

Beef Stew Mostaccioli

Bay leaves retain their shape; always remove them before serving the stew.

2 tablespoons vegetable oil
1-1/2 lbs. beef stew meat, cut in 1-inch cubes
1/2 chopped onion
1 garlic clove, pressed
1/4 cup water
2 bay leaves
3 cups beef broth
1 (8-oz.) can tomato sauce

2 tablespoons butter
1-1/2 teaspoons salt
Black pepper to taste
3 cups mostaccioli, uncooked (8 oz.)
1 (4-oz.) can peas, drained or
   1 (10-oz.) pkg. frozen peas, thawed
Grated Parmesan cheese

Heat oil in a heavy 5-quart pot or Dutch oven. Add meat, onion and garlic. Sauté until meat is browned on all sides. Add water and bay leaves. Cover and simmer 1 hour over low heat. Add beef broth, tomato sauce, butter, salt and pepper. Bring to a boil. Add mostaccioli. Bring to a boil again, stirring constantly. Cover and cook 10 minutes. Uncover; stir in peas. Cook 5 minutes longer, until mostaccioli is done. Remove bay leaves. Top with grated Parmesan cheese. Serve immediately. Makes 6 servings.

Beef Stroganoff

Once the sour cream has been added, don't let the meat mixture boil.

1-1/2 lbs. boneless sirloin, cut across grain in
   1-inch strips, 1/8 inch thick
2 tablespoons flour
1 teaspoon salt
1/8 teaspoon black pepper
3 tablespoons vegetable oil
1/2 lb. fresh mushrooms, sliced
1/2 cup chopped onion
1 small garlic clove, pressed
2 cups beef broth

1/3 cup dry sherry wine
1 tablespoon chili sauce
1 teaspoon Worcestershire sauce
1/4 teaspoon dry mustard
6 cups water
1 teaspoon salt
2 teaspoons vegetable oil
4 cups medium noodles, uncooked (8 oz.)
1 tablespoon soft butter
1/2 cup dairy sour cream

Dip meat into a mixture of 1 tablespoon flour, 1 teaspoon salt and pepper. Heat 3 tablespoons oil in a large skillet. Brown meat on both sides, about 10 minutes. Remove meat from skillet; set aside. Combine mushrooms, onion and garlic in skillet. Sauté until onion is golden. Stir in remaining 1 tablespoon flour; cook 1 minute. Stir in browned meat, beef broth, wine, chili sauce, Worcestershire sauce and mustard. Cover and simmer 45 minutes or until meat is tender. Bring water to a rapid boil in a heavy 3-quart saucepan. Add 1 teaspoon salt and 2 teaspoons oil. Gradually add noodles, being sure water continues to boil. Cook noodles uncovered until tender but firm, stirring occasionally. Drain. Toss hot cooked noodles with butter. Place on a large platter. Stir sour cream into meat mixture. Pour meat mixture over noodles. Serve immediately. Makes 4 servings.

Beef Bourguignonne

Burgundy wine is the secret.

4 slices bacon
2 lbs. beef sirloin cubes or beef chuck cubes
2 medium onions, sliced
1 garlic clove, pressed
1/2 lb. sliced fresh mushrooms
1 (10-1/2-oz.) can condensed beef broth
1 cup water
1 cup Burgundy wine
1 tablespoon minced fresh parsley
1/2 teaspoon salt

1/8 teaspoon black pepper
1/4 teaspoon dried thyme
1 bay leaf
1/4 cup water
1/4 cup all-purpose flour
7 cups water
1-1/2 teaspoons salt
1 tablespoon vegetable oil
5 cups medium noodles, uncooked (10 oz.)

In a large skillet or Dutch oven, cook bacon until crisp. Remove, drain and crumble bacon; set aside. Brown meat cubes in drippings. Add onions, garlic and mushrooms during last five minutes of browning. Drain off excess fat. Add crumbled bacon, broth, 1 cup water, wine, parsley, 1/2 teaspoon salt, pepper, thyme and bay leaf. Cover and cook 1 hour until tender. Remove bay leaf. Blend 1/4 cup water and flour. Slowly stir flour mixture into meat mixture. Cook and stir until thickened. Bring 7 cups water to a rapid boil in a heavy 5-quart pot. Add 1-1/2 teaspoons salt and oil. Gradually add noodles, being sure water continues to boil. Cook noodles uncovered until tender but firm, stirring occasionally. Drain. Serve meat mixture over hot cooked noodles. Makes 6 servings.

Steak Supreme

Mostaccioli—small moustaches—are 2-inch long tubes cut diagonally.

1/2 cup Clarified Butter, see below
2 (1-lb.) Porterhouse steaks
Salt and pepper to taste
3 green onions, thinly sliced
4 oz. fresh mushrooms, sliced
1/4 cup dry white wine

3/4 cup half-and-half
6 cups water
1 teaspoon salt
2 teaspoons vegetable oil
4 cups mostaccioli, uncooked (8 oz.)
Grated Parmesan cheese

Clarified Butter:
1/2 lb. butter, salted or unsalted

Clarify Butter. Measure 1/2 cup. Store remaining Clarified Butter for another use. Heat 1/4 cup Clarified Butter in a large skillet. Add steaks. Sear 3 to 4 minutes on each side; reduce heat so butter is hot but not burning. For medium-rare steaks, turn when red juices appear on the surface. For well-done steaks, brown another 2 to 3 minutes on each side. Season steaks with salt to taste and pepper and place on a hot platter. Add remaining 1/4 cup Clarified Butter to skillet. Sauté onions and mushrooms until onions are golden, about 5 minutes. Add wine. Cook until wine evaporates, stirring often. Slowly stir in half-and-half. Heat through, about 1 to 2 minutes. While steaks are cooking, bring water to a rapid boil in a heavy 3-quart saucepan. Add 1 teaspoon salt and oil. Gradually add mostaccioli, being sure water continues to boil. Cook mostaccioli uncovered until tender but firm, stirring occasionally. Drain. Place in a warm serving bowl. Stir in half-and-half mixture. Sprinkle with Parmesan cheese. Serve immediately with steaks. Makes 4 servings.

Clarified Butter:
Melt butter in a heavy saucepan over medium-low heat. The butter will separate into 3 parts: a watery layer on the bottom, a large amount of butter oil in the middle, and a white protein layer on top. Boil the butter until the watery portion evaporates and the white fluffy portion becomes granulated. Do not brown. Strain oil, or Clarified Butter, into a jar. Cover and refrigerate. Store several weeks in the refrigerator or freeze for long storage. Makes about 3/4 cup Clarified Butter.

Quick Chili Beef

Put this favorite together in less than 30 minutes.

1 lb. lean ground beef
1/2 cup chopped onion
2 tablespoons chopped green pepper
1 qt. tomato juice (32 oz.)
2 cups water

1 teaspoon salt
1 teaspoon chili powder
4 cups thin noodles, uncooked (8 oz.)
1 (16-oz.) can peas or beans, drained or
1 (10-oz.) pkg. frozen peas or beans, cooked

In a heavy 4-quart pan or Dutch oven, brown meat, onion and green pepper, stirring to break up meat. Add tomato juice, water, salt and chili powder. Bring to a boil. Stir in noodles. Bring to a boil again. Cover and simmer 10 minutes until noodles are tender, stirring once. Stir in peas or beans during last 2 minutes of cooking to heat through. Serve immediately. Makes 6 servings.

Cheese & Hamburg Pie

Egg, cooked noodles and cheese make a tasty crust.

Beef Filling, see below
4 cups water
1/2 teaspoon salt
1 teaspoon vegetable oil
2 cups medium noodles, uncooked (4 oz.)

1 tablespoon milk
1 tablespoon soft butter
7 slices processed American cheese
1 egg, slightly beaten

Beef Filling:

1 lb. lean ground beef
1 small onion, chopped
1 cup chopped celery
1 (8-oz.) can tomato sauce

1 teaspoon salt
Black pepper to taste
1/4 teaspoon dried oregano

Prepare Beef Filling. Set aside and keep hot. Butter a 9-inch pie plate; set aside. Bring water to a rapid boil in a heavy 2-quart saucepan. Add salt and oil. Gradually add noodles, being sure water continues to boil. Cook noodles uncovered until tender but firm, stirring occasionally. Drain. Add milk, butter, 2 slices cheese cut in julienne strips and egg. Mix well. Press into prepared pie plate. Place pie plate in cold oven. Set temperature control at 400°F (205°C). Bake 8 minutes. Remove from oven. Place 2 slices cheese on top of hot noodle shell. Spoon hot Beef Filling over cheese. Cut remaining 3 slices cheese into triangles. Arrange on top of meat filling. Return to oven. Bake until cheese melts, 2 minutes longer. Cut in wedges and serve hot. Makes 6 servings.

Beef Filling:

In a large skillet, brown meat, onion and celery about 10 minutes, stirring to break up meat. Stir in tomato sauce, salt, pepper and oregano. Cook until thickened, stirring occasionally.

Most pasta package directions give a time range for cooking. Start testing the pasta at the shortest time indicated to avoid overcooking.

Beef Rouladen

Tiny pearl macaroni is also called perline *and is often used in soups.*

1-1/2 lbs. bottom round steak,
   sliced 1/8 inch thick, cut into 6" x 3" pieces
1/2 teaspoon salt
1/8 teaspoon black pepper
1-1/2 cups water
1/4 teaspoon salt
1/2 teaspoon vegetable oil
1/4 cup tiny pearl macaroni

1 green onion, thinly sliced
2 tablespoons minced celery
4 tablespoons butter
Black pepper to taste
1 tablespoon grated Parmesan cheese
2 cups beef broth
1 tablespoon flour
2 tablespoons water

Sprinkle meat with 1/2 teaspoon salt and 1/8 teaspoon pepper; set aside. Bring 1-1/2 cups water to a rapid boil in a heavy 2-quart saucepan. Add 1/4 teaspoon salt and oil. Gradually add pearl macaroni, being sure water continues to boil. Cook macaroni uncovered until tender but firm, stirring occasionally. Drain. In a small skillet, cook onion and celery in 2 tablespoons butter until onion is golden. Do not brown. Remove from heat. Stir in cooked tiny pearl macaroni, pepper to taste and Parmesan cheese. Mix well. Spread stuffing mixture evenly over steak pieces. Roll up like a jelly roll and tie with a string. In the same skillet, brown meat rolls evenly on all sides in remaining 2 tablespoons butter. Pour broth over meat rolls. Cover and simmer 1 hour, turning occasionally. Place meat on a warm platter. Cut and remove strings. Mix flour with 2 tablespoons water. Stir into hot gravy. Cook and stir until thickened. Pour over beef rolls, serve immediately. Makes 6 servings.

Turkey Tetrazzini

It's easy to mix the sauce with the pasta if you do it in the pot the pasta is cooked in.

1/2 lb. fresh mushrooms, sliced
6 tablespoons butter
2 tablespoons flour
1 teaspoon salt
1-1/2 cups half-and-half
1 cup chicken broth
2 egg yolks
1/3 cup dry white wine

3 qts. water
1 tablespoon salt
1 tablespoon vegetable oil
1/2 lb. thin spaghetti or vermicelli,
   uncooked
2 cups cubed cooked turkey
1 cup shredded Cheddar or Swiss cheese (4 oz.)

Butter a 13" x 9" baking dish; set aside. In a medium skillet, sauté mushrooms in 2 tablespoons butter about 10 minutes; set aside. Melt remaining 4 tablespoons butter in a saucepan. Stir in flour and 1 teaspoon salt. Stir and cook until bubbly. Add half-and-half and broth. Cook and stir until thickened. In a small bowl, beat egg yolks. Gradually stir about 1 cup hot sauce into beaten egg yolks. Blend yolk mixture into hot sauce. Add wine. Heat through. Bring water to a rapid boil in a heavy 5-quart pot or Dutch oven. Add 1 tablespoon salt and oil. Gradually add spaghetti or vermicelli, being sure water continues to boil. Cook pasta uncovered until tender but firm, stirring occasionally. Drain. Return pasta to dry cooking pot. Add 1-1/2 cups sauce; mix with cooked spaghetti or vermicelli. Arrange mixture in prepared baking dish, making a well in the center. Add turkey and sautéed mushrooms to remaining sauce. Spoon into well. Sprinkle with shredded cheese. Cover and place in cold oven. Set temperature control at 400°F (205°C). Bake 20 minutes. Makes 4 servings.

Milwaukee-Style Beef & Beer

Beer adds a different and delightful flavor as it tenderizes the beef.

2 tablespoons vegetable oil
1-1/2 lbs. lean beef rump or chuck,
   cut in 1-inch cubes
2-1/2 cups thinly sliced onions
3/4 cup beef broth
1 tablespoon brown sugar
1 large garlic clove, pressed
1 tablespoon chopped fresh parsley
1 bay leaf
1 teaspoon salt

1/4 teaspoon dried thyme
1/4 teaspoon black pepper
1 (12-oz.) bottle beer, room temperature
2 quarts water
1-1/2 teaspoons salt
1 tablespoon oil
5 cups medium noodles, uncooked (10 oz.)
1 tablespoon cornstarch
1 tablespoon water
1 tablespoon poppy seeds for garnish

Heat 2 tablespoons oil in a large skillet. Add beef cubes and brown on all sides. Remove beef cubes; set aside. Sauté onions in pan drippings until tender and golden. Add broth, brown sugar, garlic, parsley, bay leaf, 1 teaspoon salt, thyme and pepper. Bring to a boil. Return cooked beef to pan. Pour beer over meat. Cover and simmer about 1-1/2 hours until meat is tender. Bring 2 quarts water to a rapid boil in a heavy 4-quart saucepan. Add 1-1/2 teaspoons salt and 1 tablespoon oil. Gradually add noodles, being sure water continues to boil. Cook noodles uncovered until tender but firm, stirring occasionally. Drain. Place in a large serving dish. Keep warm. In a small bowl, blend cornstarch and water to make a paste. Slowly stir paste into meat mixture. Cook until thickened, stirring occasionally, about 5 minutes. Remove bay leaf. Serve over hot cooked noodles. Sprinkle with poppy seeds. Makes 4 to 6 servings.

Manicotti With Tomato Sauce

If you buy manicotti tubes, use the variation below.

1 (10-oz.) pkg. frozen chopped spinach
Water
1/2 lb. lean ground beef
1/2 lb. bulk Italian sausage
1/4 cup chopped onion

2 eggs
1/4 cup grated Parmesan cheese
1/4 teaspoon salt
12 cooked Manicotti, page 20
2 cups Classic Tomato Sauce, page 138

Cook spinach in water following package directions. Drain well. In a large skillet, brown ground beef, sausage and onion, stirring to break up meat. Set aside. In a medium bowl, beat eggs. Stir in Parmesan cheese and salt. Add cooked spinach and meat mixture. Place about 1/4 cup filling down center of each cooked manicotti. Fold to overlap edges. Spread about 1/4 cup Classic Tomato Sauce over bottom of a shallow 13" x 9" baking dish. Place filled manicotti in dish seam-side down. Spoon 2 tablespoons Classic Tomato Sauce over each filled manicotti. Place baking dish in cold oven. Set temperature control at 350°F (175°C). Bake 20 minutes. Serve immediately. Makes 12 manicotti.

Variation

Substitute purchased manicotti tubes for the cooked manicotti and stuff them with the beef filling. Substitute prepared Italian-style marinara sauce for Classic Tomato Sauce.

7-Decker Dinner

Serve crisp raw vegetable sticks to complete this meal.

1 lb. ground beef
2 carrots, sliced thin
1 medium onion, thinly sliced,
   separated in rings
1 green pepper, cut in thin rings
5 cups water
1 teaspoon salt
2 teaspoons vegetable oil

3 cups wide noodles, uncooked (6 oz.)
4 slices American cheese, cut in thin strips
1 (16-oz.) can tomatoes, cut up
1 cup tomato juice
1/2 teaspoon Worcestershire sauce
1 teaspoon salt
Garlic salt to taste
Black pepper to taste

Brown meat in a large skillet. Drain off all but 2 tablespoons drippings. Sauté carrots in reserved drippings 5 minutes. Add onion rings and green pepper rings. Sauté 2 minutes longer and set aside. Bring water to a rapid boil in a heavy 3-quart saucepan. Add 1 teaspoon salt and oil. Gradually add noodles, being sure water continues to boil. Cook noodles uncovered until tender but firm, stirring occasionally. Drain. Butter an 11" x 7" baking pan. Layer ingredients in the following order: cooked noodles, half the cheese strips, sautéed onion, browned meat, sautéed carrots, sautéed green pepper and tomatoes. In a small bowl, combine tomato juice, Worcestershire sauce, 1 teaspoon salt, garlic salt and pepper. Pour evenly over casserole. Place casserole in cold oven. Set temperature control at 350°F (175°C). Bake 20 minutes. During last 5 minutes, place remaining cheese slices on casserole. Heat until cheese melts. Let stand 5 minutes before serving. Makes 6 servings.

How To Make 7-Decker Dinner

1/Arrange ingredients in layers: noodles, half the cheese, onion, beef, carrots, green pepper rings and tomatoes. Mix tomato juice and spices and pour over casserole.

2/During last 5 minutes of baking, place cheese slices on top of casserole. Let casserole stand 5 minutes before serving to absorb juices.

Herbed Chicken Dinner

Try the fusilli or the linguine to sample the different shapes.

1/4 cup vegetable oil
Juice of 1 lemon (about 2-1/2 tablespoons)
1 (2-1/2-lb.) broiler-fryer chicken,
  cut in pieces
6 tablespoons butter, melted
3/4 cup firmly packed fresh parsley leaves
1 small garlic clove, cut in half
1/2 teaspoon salt
1 teaspoon dried oregano

1/4 teaspoon dried basil
1/4 teaspoon dried thyme
Black pepper to taste
3 qts. water
1 tablespoon salt
1 tablespoon vegetable oil
8 oz. spaghetti, fusilli or
  linguine, uncooked

In a small bowl, beat 1/4 cup oil and lemon juice with a fork. Pour over chicken pieces. Toss to coat evenly. Refrigerate. In a blender or food processor, combine butter, parsley leaves, garlic, 1/2 teaspoon salt, oregano, basil, thyme and pepper. Cover and blend at high speed a few seconds until parsley is minced. Set aside. Broil chicken pieces skin-side up about 8-inches from heat 20 minutes or until golden brown. Turn and broil 20 minutes longer, until golden brown. During last 4 minutes of broiling, brush both sides of chicken pieces with 1/4 cup herb mixture. At the time chicken pieces are turned, bring water to a rapid boil in a heavy 5-quart pot or Dutch oven. Add 1 tablespoon salt and 1 tablespoon oil. Gradually add spaghetti, fusilli or linguine, being sure water continues to boil. Cook pasta uncovered until tender but firm, stirring occasionally. Drain. Place cooked pasta in a hot serving dish. Toss with remaining herb mixture. Arrange chicken pieces around edge of casserole. Serve immediately. Makes 4 servings.

Chicken In-A-Pan

Ditalini—little thimbles—are short straight macaroni. Elbow macaroni can be substituted.

1 (2-1/2 lb.) broiler-fryer chicken,
  cut in pieces
1 tablespoon lemon juice
1 teaspoon salt
Black pepper to taste
1 teaspoon dried tarragon
2 tablespoons butter
2 tablespoons vegetable oil

2 cups peeled diced tomatoes
2 medium onions, sliced, separated in rings
1 green pepper, cut in strips
1-1/2 cups chicken broth
1/2 cup Chablis white wine or
  additional chicken broth
1/4 cup tomato paste
1 cup ditalini macaroni (2 oz.)

Sprinkle chicken with lemon juice, salt, pepper and tarragon. In a large skillet, heat butter and oil. Brown chicken slowly on all sides. Add tomatoes, onion rings, green pepper strips, 1/2 cup chicken broth, wine and tomato paste. Cover and bring to a boil over high heat. Reduce heat and simmer about 45 minutes until chicken is tender. Remove chicken and keep warm. Add remaining 1 cup broth to the vegetables; bring to a boil. Stir in macaroni. Bring to a boil again, stirring constantly. Reduce heat and cook 10 minutes. Place chicken in center of a warm platter. Arrange macaroni around chicken. Serve immediately. Makes 6 servings.

How To Make Chicken Kiev

1/Shape butter into 2-inch rolls. Twirl butter rolls in prepared herb seasoning mix and freeze for 30 minutes.

2/Place each chicken breast between 2 pieces of waxed paper. With a mallet, flatten breasts until they are 1/4 inch thick.

3/Place a frozen butter roll in the center of each flattened chicken breast. Carefully fold chicken to completely enclose butter roll. Secure with a wooden pick before dipping in flour, egg and breadcrumbs.

Chicken Kiev

Make breadcrumbs in your blender. Dry them in a 250°F (120°C) oven 30 minutes.

1/4 lb. butter
2 tablespoons chopped chives
2 tablespoons chopped fresh parsley
2 teaspoons dried tarragon
1/2 teaspoon dried rosemary, crushed
1/2 teaspoon dried oregano
Garlic powder to taste
4 whole chicken breasts (about 2-1/2 lbs.),
    split, skinned, boned
1/4 cup flour
1 egg, beaten

1/2 cup dry breadcrumbs
Oil for deep-frying
Salt to taste
Freshly ground black pepper to taste
6 cups water
1 teaspoon salt
2 teaspoons vegetable oil
4 cups thin noodles, uncooked (8 oz.)
4 tablespoons soft butter
Grated Romano cheese

Cut a stick of butter in half crosswise. Cut and shape each half into 8 rolls about 1/2 inch thick. In a small bowl, mix chives, parsley, tarragon, rosemary, oregano and garlic powder. Twirl butter rolls in mixed herbs. Place butter rolls in freezer 30 minutes. To flatten chicken breasts, pound them between 2 pieces of waxed paper until they are 1/4 inch thick. Preheat deep-frying oil in deep-fryer or heavy deep skillet to 350°F (175°C). At this temperature a 1-inch cube of bread will turn golden brown in 65 seconds. Place 1 frozen butter roll in the center of each half breast. Carefully fold so butter roll is completely enclosed. Secure with a wooden pick. Roll chicken in flour, dip in beaten egg, then roll in breadcrumbs. Repeat with remaining chicken and butter rolls. Deep-fry in oil about 5 minutes until chicken is golden. Drain on paper towels. Season with salt and pepper to taste. Bring water to a rapid boil in a heavy 3-quart saucepan. Add 1 teaspoon salt and 2 teaspoons vegetable oil. Gradually add noodles, being sure water continues to boil. Cook noodles uncovered until tender but firm, stirring occasionally. Drain. Toss cooked noodles with 4 tablespoons butter. Sprinkle with Romano cheese. Serve immediately with Chicken Kiev. Makes 6 to 8 servings.

Sophie's Kapama Olympian

Punch holes in the onion with a metal skewer and the cloves will slide into the onion easier.

1 (2-lb.) leg of lamb, cut in serving pieces	1 medium onion
Juice of 1 lemon (about 2 tablespoons)	10 whole cloves
1-1/2 teaspoons salt	2 (2-inch) cinnamon sticks, broken
1/8 teaspoon black pepper	2 garlic cloves, cut in half
1/4 cup olive oil	1 orange
2 tablespoons all-purpose flour	6 cups mostaccioli, uncooked (3/4 lb.)
1 (6-oz.) can tomato paste	1/3 cup grated Parmesan cheese
4 cups hot water	1 lemon slice for garnish

Sprinkle lamb pieces with lemon juice, salt and pepper. Heat oil in a large heavy pot or Dutch oven. Brown lamb pieces slowly on all sides, about 20 minutes. Remove lamb pieces; set aside. Stir flour into drippings. Continue stirring until lightly browned. Mix tomato paste and hot water. Stir into flour mixture. Add browned lamb pieces. Stud onion with cloves. Place onion, cinnamon sticks and garlic on a 5-inch square piece of cheesecloth. Bring edges together and tie with a string to make a spice bag. Place spice bag in sauce. Cut orange in half. Squeeze orange juice into sauce; add orange halves to sauce. Bring mixture to a boil. Cover and reduce heat. Simmer 1 hour until lamb is tender. Remove and discard spice bag and orange halves. Remove lamb and keep warm. Bring sauce to a boil; add macaroni. Bring to a boil again. Cook 2 to 3 minutes stirring occasionally to keep macaroni from sticking. Continue cooking 10 to 15 minutes or until macaroni is done. Spoon onto a warm platter. Sprinkle with Parmesan cheese. Toss lightly. Arrange lamb pieces on platter with macaroni. Garnish with lemon slice. Makes 6 servings.

Variation

Substitute 2 pounds lean beef stew meat, cubed beef sirloin or 1 (2-1/2-pound) broiler-fryer chicken, cut in serving pieces, for lamb. Use 6 cups (3/4 pound) broken macaroni in place of mostaccioli.

Sophie's Kapama Olympian is pictured on the preceding pages.

Chicken Paprikash

You can also serve this combination over Bavarian Spaetzle, page 17.

1 (2-1/2-lb.) broiler-fryer chicken,
  cut in pieces
1 teaspoon salt
1/4 teaspoon black pepper
1/3 cup all-purpose flour
1 tablespoon butter
1 tablespoon shortening
1/2 cup chopped onion
1-1/4 cups chicken broth

3 tablespoons paprika
1 cup dairy sour cream
2/3 cup shredded carrot
1/4 cup butter
6 cups water
1 teaspoon salt
2 teaspoons vegetable oil
4 cups medium noodles, uncooked (8 oz.)

Sprinkle chicken pieces with 1 teaspoon salt and pepper. Dip in flour to coat all sides. Heat 1 tablespoon butter and shortening in a large skillet. Slowly brown chicken pieces on both sides. Add onion during last few minutes of browning. Drain off excess fat. Pour chicken broth over browned chicken. Sprinkle with paprika. Bring to a boil over high heat. Reduce heat. Cover and simmer 50 to 60 minutes until chicken is tender. Gradually stir in sour cream. In a small skillet, sauté shredded carrot in 1/4 cup butter. Bring water to a rapid boil in a heavy 3-quart saucepan. Add 1 teaspoon salt and oil. Gradually add noodles, being sure water continues to boil. Cook noodles uncovered until tender but firm, stirring occasionally. Drain. Return cooked noodles to dry cooking pot. Add carrots to cooked noodles. Toss together. Place on a large warmed platter. Arrange chicken pieces over noodles. Pour sauce over chicken and noodles. Makes 4 servings.

Country Chicken

Home cooking at its best.

2 tablespoons vegetable oil
1 tablespoon lemon juice
2 teaspoons dried oregano
1 teaspoon salt
1/4 teaspoon black pepper
1 garlic clove, pressed
1 (2-1/2-lb.) broiler-fryer chicken,
  cut in pieces

1 tablespoon butter
1 (16-oz.) can stewed tomatoes, cut up
1 (8-oz.) can tomato sauce
3-1/2 cups hot water
1/2 teaspoon salt
10 oz. thin spaghetti, broken in half
Grated Parmesan or Romano cheese
  for garnish

Preheat oven to 400°F (200°C). Beat oil, lemon juice, oregano, 1 teaspoon salt, pepper and garlic until mixed well but not frothy. Coat chicken with oil mixture. Place chicken skin side down in a small heavy roasting pan. Dot with butter. In a small bowl, combine stewed tomatoes, tomato sauce and 1/2 cup hot water. Spoon tomato mixture over chicken. Bake in preheated oven, 30 minutes. Turn chicken and bake 20 minutes longer. Remove chicken and pan from oven and place on surface unit of stove. Remove chicken from pan. Set aside and keep warm. Stir remaining 3 cups hot water into pan drippings. Add 1/2 teaspoon salt. Bring to a boil. Stir in spaghetti. Cook about 15 minutes, stirring often. Place on large warm platter surrounded by chicken. Sprinkle with grated cheese. Serve immediately. Makes 4 servings.

Butterfly Pasta With Pork Patties

For variety, try this with ground beef.

1 lb. coarsely ground lean pork
1-1/2 cups soft breadcrumbs
1/2 cup chopped onion
2 eggs, slightly beaten
2 tablespoons dry white wine
1 tablespoon minced fresh parsley
1 garlic clove, pressed
1 teaspoon salt
1/4 teaspoon dried mint leaves
Black pepper to taste

Cinnamon to taste
Vegetable oil for frying
Flour for coating pork patties
Tomato Sauce, see below
2 qts. water
1-1/2 teaspoons salt
2 teaspoons vegetable oil
5 cups butterfly or bow shaped pasta,
   uncooked (10 oz.)

Tomato Sauce:
1 (15-oz.) can tomato sauce with onion,
   green pepper
1/2 cup water
1 tablespoon reserved drippings
2 teaspoons butter

1/2 teaspoon salt
1/4 teaspoon dried oregano
Cinnamon to taste
Black pepper to taste

In a medium bowl, combine ground pork, breadcrumbs, onion, eggs, wine, parsley, garlic, 1 teaspoon salt, mint leaves, pepper and cinnamon. Heat oil for frying in a large skillet. Shape meat mixture into 18 small patties. Coat with flour. Fry over medium heat until brown, about 10 minutes on each side. Reserve 1 tablespoon drippings for sauce. Set patties aside and keep warm. Prepare Tomato Sauce. Preheat oven to 375°F (175°C). Bring water to a rapid boil in a heavy 4-quart saucepan. Add 1-1/2 teaspoons salt and 2 teaspoons oil. Gradually add butterflies or bows, being sure water continues to boil. Cook pasta uncovered until tender but firm, stirring occasionally. Drain. Place in a large baking dish. Arrange meat patties on top of pasta. Spoon Tomato Sauce over patties and pasta. Bake in preheated oven 20 minutes. Serve immediately. Makes 4 to 6 servings.

Tomato Sauce:
In a small saucepan combine all ingredients and heat through. Makes 2-1/2 cups.

Garnish pasta with an uncooked sauce ingredient such as a broccoli floweret, mushrooms or green pepper rings.

Ravioli

You can substitute canned spaghetti sauce for Classic Tomato Sauce.

Chicken Filling, see below or
  Meat Filling, page 114
2 cups Classic Tomato Sauce, page 138
Egg Noodle Pasta dough, page 14

4 qts. water
1 tablespoon salt
Grated Parmesan cheese, if desired

Chicken Filling:

1-1/2 cups minced cooked chicken
3 tablespoons grated Parmesan cheese
1 egg
1 tablespoon minced fresh parsley
1 tablespoon snipped chives

1/2 teaspoon grated lemon peel
1/2 teaspoon salt
1/8 teaspoon black pepper
1 tablespoon soft butter

Prepare Chicken Filling or Meat Filling; refrigerate. Prepare Classic Tomato Sauce. Divide pasta dough into 6 balls. If using a pasta machine, roll out immediately. If rolling out by hand, place dough in a plastic bag; let rest 1 hour. On a lightly floured surface, roll out 2 balls of dough into two 13" x 5" rectangles, 1/8 inch thick. On 1 of the rectangles, place Chicken Filling by rounded teaspoonfuls in 2 rows of 6 mounds each. Mounds should be about 2 inches apart. Cover with the second pasta rectangle. Use your fingers to press around each mound of filling. With a pastry cutter, cut between the mounds to make 12 squares. If using a knife to cut between the squares, press with a fork to seal edges after cutting. Repeat with remaining 2 balls of dough. **If using a ravioli form,** place 1 pasta rectangle over the indented tray. Place plastic insert onto dough to make indentations. Remove insert. Place about 1 rounded teaspoon filling into each indentation. Place another pasta rectangle over the top. With a rolling pin, roll firmly back and forth over fluted edges of the indented tray to trim off excess dough and cut into squares. Remove individual ravioli from tray, checking that edges are sealed. Repeat with remaining 4 rolls of pasta dough. Place ravioli on a lightly floured cloth towel to dry before cooking, 1 to 1-1/2 hours. Bring water and salt to a boil in a heavy 5-quart pot. Add 9 ravioli. Bring water to a boil again. Cook gently about 5 minutes until edges of pasta are tender. Drain well. Repeat with remaining ravioli. Layer ravioli on a warm platter. Pour hot Classic Tomato Sauce over ravioli. Serve with grated Parmesan cheese, if desired. Makes about 6 servings.

Chicken Filling:
Mix all ingredients in a small bowl.

Variations

Substitute 1-1/2 cups minced cooked turkey for the chicken.

Ravioli may also be served with 6 tablespoons butter heated until frothy and brown; pour immediately over ravioli.

Fish & Seafood

Pasta is an excellent base for stretching expensive seafood and fish into exciting main dishes that aren't extravagant.

Lemon Pasta, page 14, goes well with fish or seafood. You might not have time to make it often, but try it at least once. There's nothing like flavored pasta to add interest to a meal!

The most popular seafood sauce uses clams as the base. Both Vermicelli With Red Clam Sauce and Noodles With White Clam Sauce show how two cans of clams can generously serve four people. Either sauce can be put together in about 30 minutes.

As you prepare lemons for juicing or for serving in wedges, keep in mind that one lemon yields about 3 tablespoons lemon juice. To get the most juice from a lemon, soak it in hot water for 10 to 15 minutes before cutting it.

Before you are tempted to cover pasta and fish with grated Parmesan cheese, try it without. The cheese taste may overpower the delicate flavor of the fish.

Menu
Davy Jones Locker
Crab à la Cordon Bleu, page 97
Baby Peas With Mushrooms
Mixed Fruit Salad
Lemon Squares, page 155

Crab Marinara

Bright green broccoli adds color and crisp-tender texture.

2 tablespoons olive oil
1/2 cup chopped onion
1 (15-oz.) can tomato sauce
2 tablespoons chopped fresh parsley
1 tablespoon sugar
1/2 teaspoon salt
1/2 teaspoon dried basil
1/2 teaspoon dried oregano
White pepper to taste

1 (6-oz.) pkg. frozen crab, thawed, drained or
   1 (4-1/2-oz.) can small shrimp, drained
3 qts. water
1 tablespoon salt
1 tablespoon vegetable oil
1/2 lb. fusilli, fettuccini or linguine
1 (10-oz.) pkg. frozen broccoli spears
Water

Heat olive oil in a medium saucepan over low heat. Sauté onion in oil until golden. Add tomato sauce, parsley, sugar, 1/2 teaspoon salt, basil, oregano and pepper. Bring to a boil. Reduce heat and simmer 30 minutes. Stir in crab or shrimp. Bring 10 cups water to a rapid boil in a heavy 5-quart pot or Dutch oven. Add 2 teaspoons salt and 1 tablespoon oil. Gradually add fusilli, fettuccini or linguine, being sure water continues to boil. Cook pasta uncovered until tender but firm, stirring occasionally. Drain; set aside. Cook broccoli in water according to package directions. Spoon pasta into a large serving dish. Cover with 1/2 of sauce. Lay cooked broccoli spears on top of sauce. Spoon remainder of sauce over broccoli spears. Serve immediately. Makes 4 servings.

Crab à la Cordon Bleu

White pepper adds flavor without changing the color of the sauce.

2 cups chopped cooked chicken
3 slices cooked ham, cut in julienne strips
   (4 oz.)
3 slices Swiss cheese, cut in julienne strips
   (4 oz.)

6 Manicotti, page 20, cooked or
   6 manicotti tubes, cooked, drained
Crab Sauce, see below

Crab Sauce:
2 tablespoons butter
2 tablespoons all-purpose flour
3/4 cup half-and-half

1/2 cup milk
Salt and white pepper to taste
1 (6-oz.) pkg. frozen crab, thawed, drained

Butter an 11" x 7" baking dish. Divide chicken, ham and cheese evenly into 6 portions. Place in centers of Manicotti Crepes. Fold sides of crepes over filling. Spoon 1/2 cup Crab Sauce in bottom of prepared baking dish. Place filled crepes seam side down on top of sauce. Spoon remaining Crab Sauce over crepes. Cover and place in cold oven. Set temperature control at 350°F (175°C). Bake 20 minutes. Makes 6 servings.

Crab Sauce:
Melt butter in a 1-quart saucepan. Blend flour into butter. Cook until bubbly. Slowly add half-and-half and milk, salt and pepper, stirring constantly. Continue stirring until thickened. Add crab and heat thoroughly. Makes 1-1/2 cups.

Creamy Crab Sauce

Serve this rich sauce over any hot cooked pasta.

1/4 cup butter
2 tablespoons all-purpose flour
2 cups half-and-half
2 egg yolks, slightly beaten
1/2 teaspoon salt
White pepper to taste
1 tablespoon lemon juice
1 tablespoon dry white wine
1 teaspoon Worcestershire sauce

Tabasco sauce to taste
2 (6-oz.) pkgs. frozen crab,
   thawed, drained, flaked
4 qts. water
1 tablespoon salt
1 tablespoon vegetable oil
1 lb. fettuccini, fusilli, linguine or spaghetti,
   uncooked

Melt butter in a 2-quart saucepan. Stir in flour. Cook until bubbly. Add half-and-half. Cook until thickened, stirring constantly. Reduce heat and cook 2 minutes longer. Gradually stir 1/2 cup hot mixture into beaten yolks. Stir egg yolk mixture into hot sauce. Blend in 1/2 teaspoon salt, pepper, lemon juice, wine, Worcestershire sauce, Tabasco sauce and crab. Simmer until crab is heated, 5 minutes. Bring water to a rapid boil in a heavy 5-quart Dutch oven. Add 1 tablespoon salt and oil. Gradually add fettuccini, fusilli, linguine or spaghetti, being sure water continues to boil. Cook pasta uncovered until tender but firm, stirring occasionally. Drain. Serve crab sauce immediately over hot cooked pasta. Makes 6 servings.

Seafood Ono Ono

Prepare this Polynesian beauty for a festive buffet.

1 fresh pineapple	1/2 cup orzo
1/4 cup butter	2 cups milk
1 cup diced celery	1/2 teaspoon salt
1/2 cup sliced green onions	White pepper to taste
6 oz. raw scallops	1/4 cup toasted, slivered almonds
5 oz. raw shrimp	

Cut pineapple in half lengthwise through crown. Remove fruit, leaving shells intact. Core and dice fruit. Place diced fruit in colander to drain while making sauce. Melt butter in a large saucepan or skillet. Sauté celery, green onions, scallops, shrimp and orzo in butter until onion is golden, about 5 minutes. Add milk, salt and pepper; bring to a slow boil. Reduce heat to low. Cover and simmer 25 minutes until orzo is soft but not mushy. Fold in 1/2 of pineapple chunks. Spoon into pineapple shells. Place reserved pineapple chunks on top or around shells. Sprinkle with toasted almonds. Makes 4 servings.

Salmon Delight

Other milk-flavored cheeses go well with the delicate salmon flavor.

4 cups water	3 cups milk
1/2 teaspoon salt	1 teaspoon salt
1 teaspoon vegetable oil	White pepper to taste
1 cup elbow macaroni (4 oz.)	1/8 teaspon dry mustard
1/2 cup chopped onion	1/8 teaspoon Worcestershire sauce
1/2 cup chopped green pepper	1 cup shredded Gruyère or Edam cheese
3 tablespoons butter	1 (1-lb.) can salmon, drained
3 tablespoons flour	Crumb Topping, see below

Crumb Topping:
1/3 cup soft breadcrumbs
1 tablespoon butter

Bring water to a rapid boil in a heavy 2-quart saucepan. Add 1/2 teaspoon salt and oil. Gradually add macaroni, being sure water continues to boil. Cook macaroni uncovered until tender but firm, stirring occasionally. Drain; set aside. Butter a 2-quart casserole; set aside. In a medium saucepan over low heat, sauté onion and green pepper in butter until onion is golden. Stir in flour. Slowly add milk. Cook until mixture thickens, stirring constantly. Reduce heat and simmer 3 minutes. Add 1 teaspoon salt, pepper, mustard and Worcestershire sauce. Blend well. Add cheese. Stir until cheese is melted. Set aside. Remove salmon skin and bones. Fold salmon and cooked macaroni into cheese sauce. Spoon salmon mixture into casserole. Sprinkle with Crumb Topping. Place casserole in cold oven. Set temperature control at 350°F (175°C). Bake 25 minutes. Makes 4 servings.

Crumb Topping:
Melt butter in small skillet. Add breadcrumbs. Mix well.

Pasta From The Pier

Toast almond slivers only until golden, about 10 minutes. They continue to brown while cooling.

4 cups water
1/2 teaspoon salt
1 teaspoon vegetable oil
1 cup small elbow macaroni, uncooked (4 oz.)
1 tablespoon vegetable oil
1/2 cup coarsely chopped celery
3 tablespoons coarsely chopped green pepper
3 tablespoons coarsely chopped onion
1 (10-3/4-oz.) can condensed
    cream of mushroom soup
1/2 cup plain yogurt or dairy sour cream

1/3 cup sliced black olives
1/4 teaspoon salt
White pepper to taste
2 tablespoons butter, melted
1 tablespoon lemon juice
Salt and white pepper to taste
1 (1-lb.) pkg. frozen fillets of sole or haddock,
    thawed, drained
1/2 cup toasted almond slivers for garnish
Minced parsley leaves for garnish

Bring water to a rapid boil in a heavy 2-quart saucepan. Add 1/2 teaspoon salt and 1 teaspoon oil. Gradually add macaroni, being sure water continues to boil. Cook macaroni uncovered until tender but firm, stirring occasionally. Drain; set aside. Heat 1 tablespoon oil in a medium saucepan or skillet. Sauté celery, green pepper and onion in oil until tender. In a large bowl, combine cooked macaroni, sautéed vegetables, soup, yogurt or sour cream, olives, 1/4 teaspoon salt and pepper. Lightly butter an 11" x 7" baking dish. Spoon macaroni mixture into baking dish. Combine melted butter, lemon juice and salt and white pepper to taste. Brush butter mixture on both sides of fish fillets with a pastry brush. Arrange fish fillets on top of macaroni mixture. Place in cold oven. Set temperature control at 350°F (175°C). Bake 25 minutes until fillets are golden brown. Garnish with almond slivers and minced parsley. Makes 4 servings.

Vermicelli With Red Clam Sauce

Sauté means to quick-cook a vegetable, but not to brown it.

2 tablespoons olive oil
1/4 cup chopped onion
1 garlic clove, pressed
2 (8-oz.) cans clams
1 (15-oz.) can tomato sauce with bits
1/4 teaspoon black pepper

1/8 teaspoon salt
3 qts. water
1 tablespoon salt
1 tablespoon vegetable oil
1/2 lb. vermicelli, uncooked (8 oz.)

Heat olive oil in a medium saucepan. Sauté onion and garlic in olive oil until onion is golden. Drain clams; add liquid to onion mixture. Set clams aside. Stir tomato sauce, pepper and 1/8 teaspoon salt into onion mixture. Cover and bring to a boil. Reduce heat and simmer 30 minutes. Add clams and heat 5 minutes. Keep hot. Bring water to a rapid boil in a heavy 5-quart Dutch oven. Add 1 tablespoon salt and vegetable oil. Gradually add vermicelli, being sure water continues to boil. Cook vermicelli uncovered until tender but firm, stirring occasionally. Drain. Serve immediately with red clam sauce. Makes 4 servings.

Lobster Tails au Gratin

Creamy lobster mixture is mounded into lobster shells and topped with Cheddar cheese.

4 lobster tails, (about 2 lbs.)
Boiling water
1 teaspoon salt
Juice of 1/2 lemon (1-1/2 tablespoons)
2 tablespoons butter
2 green onions, thinly sliced
1 stalk celery, minced
1 (4-oz.) can mushroom stems and
   pieces, drained
1 teaspoon minced fresh parsley

1 (10-1/2-oz.) can condensed
   cream of mushroom soup
1/2 teaspoon dry mustard
2 tablespoons dry sherry wine
1/4 cup dairy sour cream
1/2 cup shredded Cheddar cheese (2 oz.)
Butter for noodles
Lemon Pasta dough, page 14
   cut in noodles, cooked, drained
Grated Parmesan cheese

Cover lobster tails with boiling water. Add 1 teaspoon salt and lemon juice. Cook 10 minutes with water at a slow boil. Remove lobster meat from shells. Keep shells intact. Cut lobster meat in 1-inch pieces. Heat butter in a medium saucepan. Sauté onion, celery, mushrooms and parsley in butter until onion is golden. Add soup, mustard, wine, sour cream and lobster pieces. Heat through, stirring frequently. Spoon mixture into shells. Top with Cheddar cheese. Broil 4 to 5 inches from heat until cheese melts. Serve immediately with hot buttered Lemon Pasta noodles topped with grated Parmesan cheese. Makes 4 servings.

Noodles With White Clam Sauce

Whether you serve it over Plain Pasta or Lemon Pasta, this sauce is a gourmet's delight.

3 tablespoons vegetable oil
1 small onion, minced
2 garlic cloves, minced
2 (8-oz.) cans minced clams
1/2 cup dry white wine
1 tablespoon minced fresh parsley

1/4 teaspoon white pepper
2 tablespoons butter
Lemon Pasta dough, page 14,
   cut in noodles, cooked, drained
Watercress sprigs for garnish

Heat oil in a large skillet. Add onion and garlic. Sauté in oil over medium heat until golden. Drain clam liquid into onion mixture. Stir in wine. Simmer about 5 minutes over medium heat. Stir in clams, parsley, pepper and butter; heat thoroughly. Pour clam sauce over hot cooked Lemon Pasta noodles. Garnish with watercress sprigs. Serve immediately. Makes 4 to 5 servings.

Variation
Substitute vermicelli, linguine or spaghetti for the Lemon Pasta noodles.

Captain's Favorite

Jumbo shells stuffed with crab, shrimp and mushrooms.

2 qts. water
1-1/2 teaspoons salt
1 tablespoon vegetable oil
12 jumbo macaroni shells, uncooked
3 tablespoons butter
1 (4-oz.) can mushrooms, drained
1-1/2 tablespoons flour
1 cup milk
1 cup half-and-half
1/4 teaspoon salt

1/8 teaspoon white pepper
2 egg yolks, slightly beaten
2 tablespoons dry sherry
1/4 teaspoon Worcestershire sauce
1 (6-oz.) pkg. frozen crab, thawed,
    drained, flaked
1 (4-1/2-oz.) can shrimp or
    4-1/2 oz. cooked shrimp
2 tablespoons chopped pimiento, drained
Grated Parmesan cheese

Bring water to a rapid boil in a heavy 4-quart saucepan. Add 1-1/2 teaspoons salt and oil. Gradually add shells, being sure water continues to boil. Cook shells uncovered until tender but quite firm, stirring occasionally. With a slotted spoon, remove shells from water. Invert shells on a dry cloth towel; drain 5 minutes. Cover to prevent drying. Melt butter in a medium saucepan. Add mushrooms. Sauté 5 minutes. Remove mushrooms and set aside. Stir flour into butter. Cook over low heat until bubbly, stirring constantly. Continuing to stir, blend milk, half-and-half, 1/4 teaspoon salt and pepper into flour mixture and cook until mixture thickens, about 5 minutes. Remove from heat. Blend 1/2 cup hot sauce into beaten egg yolks. Gradually add egg yolk mixture to remaining sauce. Stir in sherry and Worcestershire sauce. In a medium bowl, mix together crab, shrimp, sautéed mushrooms, pimiento and 3/4 cup sauce. Stuff jumbo shells with seafood mixture. Pour remaining sauce in an 11" x 7" baking dish. Arrange filled shells on sauce. Spoon a little of the sauce over each shell. Sprinkle with Parmesan cheese. Place in cold oven. Set temperature control at 350°F (175°C). Bake 20 minutes. Serve immediately. Makes 4 servings.

Variation

Substitute tuna for crab and shrimp. Add 1/4 cup chopped celery, 1/4 cup chopped green pepper, 2 tablespoons minced onion and 1 tablespoon minced parsley. Sauté celery, green pepper, onions and parsley with mushrooms. Add to sauce.

Red Tuna Sauce

Something different to serve over spaghetti.

1 tablespoon olive oil	1 (6-1/2-oz.) can tuna fish, drained
1/2 cup chopped onion	2 teaspoons drained capers, if desired
1 garlic clove, pressed	3 qts. water
1/2 lb. fresh mushrooms, sliced	1 tablespoon salt
1 (8-oz.) can tomato sauce	1 tablespoon vegetable oil
1/2 cup water	8 oz. fusilli, fettuccini or linguine, uncooked
1/8 teaspoon salt	2 tablespoons minced fresh parsley for garnish
1/4 teaspoon black pepper	

Heat olive oil in a small saucepan. Sauté onion, garlic and mushrooms in oil until onion is golden. Add tomato sauce, 1/2 cup water, 1/8 teaspoon salt and pepper. Simmer 25 minutes. Add tuna fish and capers. Cook 5 minutes. Bring 3-quarts water to a rapid boil in a heavy 5-quart Dutch oven. Add 1 tablespoon salt and vegetable oil. Gradually add fusilli, fettuccini or linguine, being sure water continues to boil. Cook pasta uncovered until tender but firm, stirring occasionally. Drain. Serve tuna sauce over hot cooked pasta. Sprinkle with minced parsley. Makes 4 servings.

How To Make Captain's Favorite

1/Drain cooked jumbo macaroni shells well before filling. Carefully spoon crab and shrimp mixture into each shell.

2/Pour remaining sauce into baking dish. Place filled shells on top of sauce. Spoon some sauce over shells. Sprinkle with Parmesan cheese before baking.

Tuna Velvet Casserole

Cream cheese adds a velvety texture.

4 cups water
1/2 teaspoon salt
1 teaspoon vegetable oil
1 cup elbow macaroni, uncooked (4 oz.)
1 (8-oz.) pkg. cream cheese, softened
1 (10-1/2-oz.) can condensed
   cream of celery soup

1 (6-1/2-oz.) can tuna fish, drained, flaked
1/4 cup chopped onion
1 (10-oz.) pkg. frozen peas & carrots, thawed
1/4 cup chopped walnuts
1/8 teaspoon salt
White pepper to taste
Paprika for garnish

Bring water to a rapid boil in a heavy 2-quart saucepan. Add 1/2 teaspoon salt and oil. Gradually add macaroni, being sure water continues to boil. Cook macaroni uncovered until tender but firm, stirring occasionally. Drain. Set aside. In a large bowl, blend cream cheese and soup. Fold in cooked macaroni, tuna, onion, peas and carrots, walnuts, 1/8 teaspoon salt and pepper. Butter a 1-1/2-quart casserole. Spoon macaroni mixture into casserole. Sprinkle with paprika. Place in cold oven. Set temperature control at 350°F (175°C). Bake 25 minutes until golden. Makes 4 servings.

Haddock With Lemon Noodles

Haddock is subtly flavored with lemon and fresh peppercorns.

Lemon-Butter Sauce, see below
4 cups water
1 tablespoon salt
2 teaspoons whole black peppercorns
1 small onion, cut in wedges
1/2 small lemon, thinly sliced
4 celery pieces, 2-inch long
1 bay leaf

2 lbs. frozen haddock or cod, partially thawed
1/4 cup melted butter
Paprika for garnish
Lemon Pasta dough, page 14,
   cut in noodles, cooked, drained
2 tablespoons butter
Dried dill weed for garnish

Lemon-Butter Sauce:
1/2 cup butter
1/4 cup freshly squeezed lemon juice

2 tablespoons minced fresh parsley

Prepare Lemon-Butter Sauce; set aside. In a medium saucepan, bring water, salt, peppercorns, onion, lemon, celery and bay leaf to a boil. Cut partially thawed haddock or cod into small pieces. Carefully place fish into boiling water mixture. Bring back to a boil. Simmer 8 to 10 minutes. Carefully remove fish from hot water with a slotted spoon. Place fish on greased broiler pan; brush with melted butter. Broil 4 inches from heat, about 3 minutes. Place broiled fish on a warm serving platter. Sprinkle with paprika. Place hot cooked lemon noodles in a serving dish. Toss noodles with 2 tablespoons butter. Sprinkle with dill weed for garnish. Serve haddock with Lemon-Butter Sauce. Makes 6 servings.

Lemon-Butter Sauce:
In a small saucepan melt butter; stir in lemon juice and parsley. Blend well. Makes 3/4 cup.

One-Dish Meals

Pasta meant for a casserole which requires baking should be undercooked by a third of the boiling time. Pasta casseroles can be refrigerated for 1 or 2 days. To reheat them, add a few tablespoons of water, broth or tomato juice if needed. Cover the baking dish and place it in a 350°F (175°C) oven until the center is bubbly. It is not necessary to preheat the oven.

If you're going to freeze a casserole, only partially cook it and then quickly cool it to room temperature by placing it in a large bowl or sink filled with cold water and ice. Most casseroles can be frozen for 1 to 3 months. The best way to thaw a frozen casserole is in the refrigerator. Because it thaws evenly, it will reheat evenly.

If you're pressed for time, prepare Spaghetti In-A-Skillet, Quick Noodle Skillet or Squash Casserole In-A-Skillet. These skillet casseroles are easy to put together and are quick-cooking.

I have also included some vegetarian or meatless casseroles. Old Fashioned Macaroni & Cheese is always popular. Meat Sauce Lasagne is ideal for a buffet. Vegetarian Moussaka was inspired by the popular Greek dish usually associated with lamb and eggplant. The eggplant is still there but this version is meatless. You may never add meat to Moussaka again!

Menu
A Meatless Dinner
Vegetarian Moussaka, page 110
Assorted Crisp Relishes
Whole-Wheat Bread
Fresh Fruit Medley
Cheese Wedges
Coffee

Squash Casserole In-A-Skillet

Orzo is a small pasta that looks like rice.

2 tablespoons vegetable oil
1 medium onion, chopped
1/4 cup orzo
2 tablespoons chopped fresh parsley
1/2 teaspoon dried dill weed
1/2 teaspoon salt

1/8 teaspoon black pepper
2/3 cup water
1 lb. summer, crookneck or zucchini squash, cut in 1/8-inch slices
1 apple, cut in wedges for garnish
2 teaspoons lemon juice

Heat oil in a medium saucepan. Sauté onion in oil until golden. Add orzo. Sauté until light brown, 2 to 3 minutes. Add parsley, dill weed, salt, pepper and water. Bring to a boil. Remove from heat. In the bottom of a large skillet, layer as follows: 1/2 the squash, 1/2 the orzo mixture, remaining squash and remaining orzo mixture. Cover and simmer over medium heat until orzo is tender, 25 minutes. Cut apple into wedges and brush with lemon juice. Spoon squash mixture into a serving dish. Arrange apple wedges around edge of dish. Serve immediately. Makes 4 servings.

Old Fashioned Macaroni & Cheese

Pour creamy Cheddar cheese sauce over tender macaroni and top it with golden breadcrumbs.

6 cups water
1 teaspoon salt
1 tablespoon vegetable oil
2 cups elbow macaroni (8 oz.)
2-1/2 cups cold milk
2 tablespoons cornstarch
1/4 cup butter or margarine
1/4 cup grated onion

1/2 teaspoon dry mustard
1/4 teaspoon Worcestershire sauce
1/4 teaspoon salt
1/8 teaspoon white pepper
1-1/2 cups shredded Cheddar cheese (6 oz.)
1 tablespoon butter or margarine
1/4 cup breadcrumbs
Tomato slices for garnish

Butter a 2-quart casserole; set aside. Bring water to a rapid boil in a heavy 4-quart saucepan. Add 1 teaspoon salt and oil. Gradually add macaroni, being sure water continues to boil. Cook macaroni uncovered until tender but firm, stirring occasionally. Drain. Place in prepared casserole. In a medium saucepan, blend milk into cornstarch. Add 1/4 cup butter or margarine, onion, mustard, Worcestershire sauce, salt and pepper. Bring to a boil over medium heat, stirring constantly. Reduce heat to low. Stir in cheese. Continue stirring until cheese melts. Spoon over macaroni. Melt 1 tablespoon butter or margarine in a small skillet. Stir breadcrumbs in melted butter to toast lightly. Sprinkle toasted breadcrumbs over casserole. Place casserole in cold oven. Set temperature control at 350°F (175°C). Bake 20 minutes until golden. Garnish with tomato slices. Makes 6 servings.

Herbed Beef Casserole

Pine nuts are also called pignolias, pignons *and* piñons.

1 lb. ground beef
1/3 cup chopped onion
1 garlic clove, pressed
2 (8-oz.) cans tomato sauce
1 tablespoon minced fresh parsley
1 teaspoon salt
1 teaspoon dried oregano
1 teaspoon Italian herbs
1/2 teaspoon dried dill weed

1/8 teaspoon black pepper
6 cups water
1 teaspoon salt
1 tablespoon vegetable oil
2 cups elbow macaroni, uncooked (8 oz.)
1/2 cup grated Parmesan cheese
3 slices mozzarella cheese, cut in 1-inch strips
1/4 cup pine nuts or sunflower seeds
Parsley sprigs for garnish

Butter a 9-inch square baking dish; set aside. In a large skillet, brown beef, onion and garlic, stirring to break up meat. Stir in tomato sauce, parsley, 1 teaspoon salt, oregano, Italian herbs, dill weed and pepper. Bring to a boil. Cover and reduce heat. Simmer meat sauce 30 minutes. While meat sauce simmers, bring water to a rapid boil in a heavy 3-quart saucepan. Add 1 teaspoon salt and oil. Gradually add macaroni, being sure water continues to boil. Cook macaroni uncovered until tender but firm, stirring occasionally. Drain. In a large bowl, combine cooked macaroni, Parmesan cheese and meat sauce. Spoon into prepared baking dish. Place in a cold oven. Set temperature control at 350°F (175°C). Bake 20 minutes. Arrange mozzarella strips over top of casserole. Top with pine nuts or sunflower seeds. Bake 5 minutes longer. Garnish with parsley sprigs. Makes 4 to 6 servings.

Noodles au Gratin

With rolls and salad, this is a light supper. Or it can be a substitute for potatoes.

3 cups water
1/2 teaspoon salt
1 teaspoon vegetable oil
1-1/2 cups small noodle squares or
   1-1/2 cups broken thin noodles
1 (10-3/4-oz.) can condensed
   Cheddar cheese soup
1/2 cup plain yogurt, room temperature

1/8 teaspoon salt
1/8 teaspoon white pepper
1/2 cup chopped celery
2 tablespoons chopped pimiento, drained or
   chopped sweet red pepper
2 tablespoons butter or margarine
1/2 cup breadcrumbs

Lightly butter an 11" x 7" baking dish; set aside. Bring water to a rapid boil in a heavy 2-quart saucepan. Add 1/2 teaspoon salt and oil. Gradually add noodle squares or broken noodles, being sure water continues to boil. Cook pasta uncovered until tender but firm, stirring occasionally. Drain; set aside. Blend soup, yogurt, 1/8 teaspoon salt and pepper in a medium bowl. Gently stir in cooked noodles, celery and pimiento or red pepper. Spoon noodle mixture into prepared baking dish. Melt butter or margarine in a small skillet. Add breadcrumbs and stir to toast. Sprinkle noodle mixture with toasted breadcrumbs. Cover and place in cold oven. Set temperature control at 375°F (190°C). Bake 20 minutes. Remove cover. Bake 10 minutes longer. Makes 6 to 8 servings.

Hearty Ham Dinner

A good way to use leftover ham.

6 cups water
1 teaspoon salt
2 teaspoons vegetable oil
4 cups wide noodles, uncooked (8 oz.)
1-1/2 cups chopped celery
1/3 cup boiling water
1 (8-oz.) pkg. cream cheese, room temperature
1/2 cup grated Parmesan cheese

1-1/4 cups milk
1 tablespoon chopped pimiento, drained
2 cups cubed cooked ham
1 (16-oz.) can green beans, drained
1 (4-oz.) can mushrooms, drained
1/8 teaspoon white pepper
2 tablespoons butter or margarine
2 teaspoons toasted sesame seeds

Bring 6 cups water to a rapid boil in a heavy 3-quart saucepan. Add salt and oil. Gradually add noodles, being sure water continues to boil. Cook noodles uncovered until tender but firm, stirring occasionally. Drain; set aside. Butter a 2-quart casserole; set aside. In a medium saucepan over medium heat, cook celery in 1/3 cup boiling water until tender, about 5 minutes. Drain. In a large bowl, blend cream cheese, Parmesan cheese and milk until smooth. Stir in cooked celery, pimiento, ham, green beans, mushrooms and white pepper. Gently stir in cooked noodles. Spoon mixture into prepared casserole. Dot with butter or margarine. Cover and place in cold oven. Set temperature control at 350°F (175°C). Bake 30 minutes; during final 10 minutes, remove cover and sprinkle casserole with toasted sesame seeds. Continue baking uncovered. Makes 6 servings.

Noodle Flip

Toast almonds on a baking sheet in a 325°F (165°C) oven about 10 minutes; stir occasionally.

6 cups water
1 teaspoon salt
2 teaspoons vegetable oil
4 cups fine egg noodles, uncooked (8 oz.)
1/2 cup half-and-half
1/4 cup minced onion
1/2 teaspoon salt

1/2 teaspoon celery salt
1/4 teaspoon black pepper
1 teaspoon butter
1 (10-oz.) pkg. frozen green beans,
 thawed, drained
1/4 cup toasted sliced almonds
2 cups shredded Cheddar cheese (8 oz.)

Bring water to a rapid boil in a heavy 3-quart saucepan. Add 1 teaspoon salt and oil. Gradually add noodles, being sure water continues to boil. Cook noodles uncovered until tender but firm, stirring occasionally. Drain. In a large bowl, mix together cooked noodles, half-and-half, onion, 1/2 tea-spoon salt, celery salt and pepper. In a large heavy skillet, melt butter over medium heat. Arrange half the noodle mixture on bottom of skillet. Place beans over noodles. Sprinkle with almonds then half the cheese. Top with remaining noodle mixture. Sprinkle with remaining cheese. Cover and simmer over low heat until bottom is golden and cheese is melted. To serve, invert skillet onto warm platter. Remove skillet. Cut Noodle Flip into wedges. Makes 6 to 8 servings.

Stir-Fried Pork Strips

Get out your wok and try my version of a Chinese dish.

3 tablespoons vegetable oil
1 large garlic clove, minced
1 tablespoon minced fresh ginger root
1 lb. lean pork, cut in thin strips
1 (10-oz.) pkg. frozen Chinese vegetables,
 thawed
1 (6-oz.) pkg. frozen pea pods, thawed
1/4 cup soy sauce
1 teaspoon wine vinegar

1/2 teaspoon sugar
1 (4-oz.) can mushrooms, drained
1/2 cup fresh bean sprouts
1 tablespoon water
2 teaspoons cornstarch
3 qts. water
1 tablespoon salt
1 tablespoon vegetable oil
8 cups thin egg noodles, uncooked (1 lb.)

In a wok or large skillet, heat 3 tablespoons oil, garlic and ginger. Add pork strips. Stir-fry over high heat until meat is browned. Reduce heat. Add Chinese vegetables, pea pods, soy sauce, vinegar and sugar. Cover. Cook until vegetables are tender, 3 minutes. Add mushrooms and bean sprouts. Stir 1 tablespoon water and cornstarch. Stir into sauce. Simmer uncovered 1 or 2 minutes longer, until bubbly and slightly thickened, stirring constantly. Bring 3 quarts water to a rapid boil in a heavy 5-quart pot or Dutch oven. Add salt and 1 tablespoon oil. Gradually add noodles, being sure water continues to boil. Cook noodles uncovered until tender but firm, stirring occasionally. Drain. Serve hot pork sauce over hot cooked noodles. Makes 4 servings.

Vegetarian Moussaka

A new version of the popular Greek dish.

1 medium eggplant
1 teaspoon salt
1/2 cup vegetable oil
1 lb. zucchini, cut lengthwise in 1/8-inch slices
2 medium onions, sliced
1 (16-oz.) can whole tomatoes
1/8 teaspoon black pepper
Garlic salt to taste
10 cups water

2 teaspoons salt
1 tablespoon oil
4 cups mostaccioli, uncooked (8 oz.)
1/4 cup milk
1 egg
1 tablespoon grated Parmesan cheese
2 tablespoons minced fresh parsley
1 cup shredded mozzarella cheese (4 oz.)

Oil a large baking sheet; set aside. Generously butter a 13" x 9" baking dish. Partially peel eggplant, leaving some lengthwise strips of peel. Slice crosswise 1/8-inch thick. Sprinkle with 1 teaspoon salt. Drain in a colander 20 minutes. Rinse with cold water to remove salt. Lightly squeeze slices to remove excess water. Place on prepared baking sheet. Drizzle 1/4 cup oil over eggplant slices. Broil until golden brown, 10 minutes on each side. Remove eggplant slices. Place lengthwise slices of zucchini on baking sheet. Drizzle with remaining 1/4 cup oil. Broil until golden brown, 10 minutes on each side. Remove zucchini. Pour excess oil into a small skillet. Add onions; sauté until golden; set aside. Drain tomatoes, reserving juice. Slice tomatoes. Add pepper and garlic salt to reserved juice; set aside. Bring water to a rapid boil in a heavy 5-quart pot or Dutch oven. Add 2 teaspoons salt and 1 tablespoon oil. Gradually add mostaccioli, being sure water continues to boil. Cook mostaccioli uncovered until tender but firm, stirring occasionally. Drain. Pour milk into a small bowl. Add egg and beat with a fork or whisk until mixed well but not frothy. Pour over cooked mostaccioli. Mix well. Layer in the following order: mostaccioli mixture, Parmesan cheese, broiled eggplant, sautéed onions, parsley, broiled zucchini, sliced tomatoes, tomato juice mixture and mozzarella cheese. Place baking dish in cold oven. Set temperature control at 350°F (175°C). Bake 30 minutes. Let stand 10 minutes before cutting. Makes 6 main-dish servings or 12 vegetable servings.

Conserve Energy

Casserole-type dishes do not need to be cooked in a preheated oven as baked goods such as breads and cakes do. To help you conserve energy, many of the recipes in this book instruct you to place a casserole in the cold oven then turn the oven temperature control to the desired setting. At the end of the time indicated in the recipe, the casserole will be heated through without the usual loss of energy that occurs when you preheat your oven.

How To Make
Vegetarian Moussaka

1/Using a sharp knife or potato peeler, partially peel eggplant. Slice crosswise 1/8 inch thick and sprinkle with salt. After 10 minutes, rinse and drain. Drizzle with oil before broiling.

2/Cut zucchini lengthwise into 1/8-inch thick slices and place on an oiled baking sheet. Drizzle with oil before broiling.

3/Place cooked mostaccioli in bottom of buttered baking dish. Top with Parmesan cheese, eggplant, onions, parsley, zucchini and tomato slices. Pour tomato juice mixture over the top and sprinkle with shredded mozzarella cheese.

Brussels Sprouts Cheese Bake

Partially thawed brussels sprouts will be easier to slice than either frozen or thawed.

1 lb. lean ground beef
1/2 cup chopped onion
1 (15-oz.) can tomato sauce
1 cup water
1 teaspoon sugar
3/4 teaspoon salt
1/4 teaspoon dried oregano
1/8 teaspoon black pepper
4 cups water
1/2 teaspoon salt

1 teaspoon vegetable oil
1 cup elbow macaroni, uncooked (4 oz.)
2 (10-oz.) pkgs. frozen brussels sprouts,
 partially thawed
1/4 to 1/2 cup water
1 cup creamed cottage cheese
1 egg, slightly beaten
1/4 lb. sliced mozzarella cheese (4 oz.)
1/4 cup chopped walnuts

In a large skillet over medium heat, brown meat and onion 10 minutes, stirring to break up meat. Add tomato sauce, 1 cup water, sugar, 3/4 teaspoon salt, oregano and pepper. Bring to a boil. Reduce heat to low; simmer 10 minutes, stirring occasionally. While sauce is cooking, bring 4 cups water to a rapid boil in a heavy 2-quart saucepan. Add 1/2 teaspoon salt and oil. Gradually add macaroni, being sure water continues to boil. Cook macaroni uncovered until tender but firm, stirring occasionally. Drain. Butter an 11" x 7" baking dish; set aside. Slice brussels sprouts lengthwise 1/4 inch thick. In a medium saucepan, bring 1/4 to 1/2 cup water to a boil. Add halved brussels sprouts. Cook over medium heat 5 to 7 minutes. Drain. Layer half the cooked macaroni in the bottom of the prepared baking dish. Place half the cooked brussels sprouts over the macaroni. Spoon half the meat sauce over brussels sprouts. Layer remaining cooked macaroni over meat sauce. In a small bowl, mix cottage cheese with egg. Spread cottage cheese mixture over macaroni. Layer with remaining brussels sprouts, mozzarella cheese slices and remaining meat sauce. Sprinkle with chopped walnuts. Place in a cold oven. Set temperature control at 375°F (190°C). Bake 40 minutes. Let stand 10 minutes before cutting. Makes about 6 servings.

Egg Special

Egg and zucchini team up with mostaccioli.

3 tablespoons butter
1/2 cup chopped onion
1 (8-oz.) can tomato sauce
2-1/2 cups water
2 garlic cloves, pressed
1 teaspoon salt
1 teaspoon sugar

1/4 teaspoon dried dill weed
1/8 teaspoon dried oregano
1/8 teaspoon black pepper
1 cup mostaccioli
2 lbs. zucchini, cut in 1-inch cubes
4 eggs, beaten
1/2 cup crushed corn chips

In a large skillet, melt butter over medium heat. Sauté onion in butter until golden. Add tomato sauce, water, garlic, salt, sugar, dill weed, oregano and pepper. Bring to a boil. Add mostaccioli. Bring back to a boil, stirring often. Add zucchini cubes. Cover. Cook over medium heat 20 minutes or until tender but firm. Pour eggs over top. Cover. Cook 2 to 3 minutes longer until eggs are set. Top with crushed corn chips. Serve immediately. Makes 4 servings.

Sausage & Cheese Squares

Polish sausage spices up this dinner-in-a-dish.

1 tablespoon butter
1 lb. Polish sausage or Knackwurst, sliced
1/4 cup coarsley chopped celery
2 tablespoons minced onion
5 cups water
1 teaspoon salt
1 teaspoon vegetable oil

3 cups medium noodles, uncooked (6 oz.)
2 eggs, slightly beaten
2 cups milk
1/2 teaspoon salt
1 tablespoon minced fresh parsley
3/4 cup grated Monterey Jack cheese (3 oz.)
1 tomato, cut in wedges for garnish

Butter a 9-inch square baking dish; set aside. Melt butter in a medium skillet. Sauté sausage, celery and onion until onion is golden. Bring water to a rapid boil in a heavy 4-quart saucepan. Add 1 teaspoon salt and oil. Gradually add noodles, being sure water continues to boil. Cook noodles uncovered until tender but firm, stirring occasionally. Drain. In a large bowl, combine sautéed sausage mixture, eggs, milk, 1/2 teaspoon salt and parsley. Gently stir in noodles. Spoon into prepared baking dish. Place casserole in cold oven. Set temperature control at 350°F (175°C). Bake 55 minutes. Remove casserole from oven. Sprinkle with Monterey Jack cheese. Bake 15 minutes longer. Let stand 5 minutes before cutting into squares. Garnish with tomato wedges. Makes 4 servings.

Quick Noodle Skillet

Inexpensive and quick. Use the remaining mandarin orange sections in a fruit salad.

1 lb. ground beef
1/2 cup chopped onion
1/2 cup chopped celery
1/4 cup chopped green pepper
2 cups water
2 cups beef broth
2 teaspoons salt

1/8 teaspoon black pepper
1 small garlic clove, pressed
4 cups medium egg noodles, uncooked (8 oz.)
1 (8-oz.) can water chestnuts, drained, sliced
1 (4-oz.) can pimientos, chopped, drained
1/2 (11-oz.) can mandarin orange sections, drained

In a large skillet, sauté ground beef, onion, celery and green pepper over medium heat, stirring to break up meat. Remove mixture from skillet; set aside. Pour water and broth into skillet. Add salt, pepper and garlic. Bring to a boil. Slowly add noodles. Cover and simmer until noodles are tender but firm, stirring occasionally. Stir meat mixture, water chestnuts and pimiento into cooked noodles. Heat to serving temperature, stirring occasionally. Spoon into a large serving dish. Top with mandarin orange sections. Serve immediately. Makes 4 to 6 servings.

Cappelletti

Little hats *is the translation of the Italian title.*

Meat Filling, see below
Egg Noodle Pasta dough, page 14
4 qts. water

1 tablespoon salt
2 cups Classic Tomato Sauce, page 138
Grated Parmesan cheese

Meat Filling:
1/2 lb. ground beef
1 egg, slightly beaten
1/4 cup breadcrumbs
2 tablespoons grated Parmesan cheese
1 tablespoon minced fresh parsley
1 teaspoon grated onion

1/2 teaspoon salt
1/2 teaspoon dried basil
1/2 teaspoon lemon juice
1/8 teaspon black pepper
Pinch baking soda

Prepare Meat Filling; set aside. Divide Egg Noodle Pasta dough into 3 equal parts. If using pasta machine, roll out immediately. If rolling by hand, place dough in a plastic bag; let rest 1 hour before rolling on a lightly floured surface. Roll out 1/3 of the dough almost paper thin. Cut about thirty 2-1/2-inch circles. Put about 1/2 teaspoon Meat Filling in center of a circle. Dip your finger in water and moisten edges of circle. Fold the circle over until the edges almost meet; press edges. Roll the filled circle around the tip of your finger; overlap ends and press together. If ends do not hold, moisten and press again. Pinch filled top, shaping it into a little hat. Continue until all are finished, working quickly so pasta will not dry out. Let cappelletti stand 15 minutes before cooking. Bring water and salt to a boil. Add cappelletti. Bring water to a boil again. Cook gently until pasta is tender, about 8 minutes. Drain well. Place on a warm platter. Pour hot Classic Tomato Sauce over cappelletti. Serve immediately with Parmesan cheese. Makes about 90 cappelletti using pasta machine. By hand you will get less. Makes about 8 servings.

Meat Filling
In a medium bowl, mix all ingredients together.

Variations
Substitute Chicken Filling, page 95, for Meat Filling.

Cappelletti may also be served with a brown butter sauce: melt 3/4 cup butter until frothy and brown. Immediately pour over Cappelletti. Toss gently.

How To Make Cappelletti

1/Cut 2-1/2-inch circles from thinly rolled dough. Place filling in the center of each circle. Moisten edges before folding dough over.

2/Fold dough over filling, press moistened edges together. Roll folded dough around tip of your finger and press the 2 ends together. Continue until all are completed.

3/Pinch filled top to make a shape resembling a little hat. Let filled cappelletti stand 15 minutes to dry slightly before cooking.

Pizzeria Pie

No garlic press? Crush the garlic clove with the flat side of a large knife.

1 tablespoon vegetable oil
1 teaspoon butter
3 tablespoons chopped onion
2 tablespoons chopped celery
1 small garlic clove, pressed
1 (8-oz.) can tomato puree
2 tablespoons tomato paste
2 teaspoons grated Parmesan cheese
1 teaspoon dried oregano
1/2 teaspoon dried basil
1/4 teaspoon salt
1/4 teaspoon sugar

1/4 teaspoon Worcestershire sauce
Tabasco sauce to taste
4 cups water
1/2 teaspoon salt
1 teaspoon vegetable oil
1 cup elbow macaroni, uncooked (4 oz.)
1-1/2 cups shredded mozzarella cheese (6 oz.)
1/4 cup half-and-half or milk
1 egg
1/2 lb. pepperoni or pork sausage,
  cooked, drained
1 (2-oz.) can anchovies, drained, if desired

Butter a 9-inch pie plate; set aside. Heat 1 tablespoon oil and butter in a medium saucepan over medium heat. Sauté onion, celery and garlic until onion is golden. Stir in tomato puree, tomato paste, Parmesan cheese, oregano, basil, 1/4 teaspoon salt, sugar, Worcestershire sauce and Tabasco sauce. Bring to a boil. Reduce heat and simmer 15 minutes until thickened. Keep warm. Bring water to a rapid boil in a heavy 2-quart saucepan. Add 1/2 teaspoon salt and 1 teaspoon oil. Gradually add macaroni, being sure water continues to boil. Cook macaroni uncovered until tender but firm, stirring occasionally. Drain. Sprinkle 1/2 cup mozzarella cheese over macaroni. In a small bowl, blend half-and-half or milk and egg. Stir egg mixture into macaroni and cheese. Spoon into prepared pie plate. Sprinkle with another 1/2 cup mozzarella cheese. Spread tomato puree mixture over top of pizza. Place in cold oven. Set temperature control at 350°F (175°C). Bake 10 minutes. Remove from oven. Sprinkle sausage over pizza. Top with remaining 1/2 cup mozzarella cheese. Bake until cheese is melted, about 20 minutes. Let stand 5 minutes. Garnish with anchovies, if desired. Cut in wedges. Makes 4 to 6 servings.

Spaghetti In-A-Skillet

You'll find this is an easy meal to prepare at the end of a busy day.

1 lb. ground beef
1/2 cup minced onion
1 small garlic clove, pressed
1/3 cup minced green pepper
3 cups peeled and cubed tomatoes or
  1 (16-oz.) can tomatoes
2-2/3 cups water

1/2 cup ketchup
1 teaspoon salt
1/4 teaspoon dried oregano
1/4 teaspoon black pepper
8 oz. spaghetti, broken in thirds
3 slices toast, spread with garlic butter,
  for garnish

In a large skillet over medium heat, brown meat, onion and garlic, stirring to break up meat. Add green pepper. Cook 3 minutes longer. Add tomatoes, water, ketchup, salt, oregano and pepper. Bring to a boil. Add spaghetti. Bring back to a boil, stirring to separate spaghetti pieces. Reduce heat and simmer 30 minutes, stirring occasionally. Spoon into a serving dish. Cut garlic toast into triangles and arrange around edge of serving dish. Serve immediately. Makes 4 servings.

Meat Sauce Lasagne

Absolutely the most delicious lasagne ever!

Meat Sauce, see below
3 qts. water
1 tablespoon salt
1 tablespoon vegetable oil
12 strips white or green lasagne noodles

1 egg
1 (1-lb.) carton small curd cottage cheese
1/2 (1-lb.) carton ricotta cheese
1/2 cup grated Parmesan cheese
1 lb. mozzarella cheese, thinly sliced

Meat Sauce:
1-1/2 lbs. lean ground beef
1/2 cup chopped onion
1 (1-lb.) can tomato bits
1 (8-oz.) can tomato sauce
1 (6-oz.) can tomato paste
2 tablespoons dried parsley flakes
1/3 cup dry red wine
2 garlic cloves, pressed

2 teaspoons dried oregano
1 teaspoon sugar
1/4 teaspoon dried thyme
1/4 teaspoon dried marjoram
1/8 teaspoon black pepper
1/8 teaspoon cayenne pepper
Salt to taste

Prepare Meat Sauce. Butter a 13" x 9" baking dish; set aside. Bring water to a rapid boil in a heavy 5-quart pot or Dutch oven. Add salt and oil. Gradually add lasagne noodles, being sure water continues to boil. Cook noodles uncovered until tender but firm, stirring occasionally. Drain. In a medium bowl, beat egg. Stir in cottage cheese, ricotta cheese and Parmesan cheese; mix thoroughly. Place a thin layer of Meat Sauce in the prepared dish. Layer half the lasagne noodles on top of sauce. Spread half the cheese mixture over noodles. Cover with half the remaining Meat Sauce. Arrange half the mozzarella cheese slices over sauce. Repeat with remaining noodles, cheese mixture and meat mixture. Place in cold oven. Set temperature control at 375°F (190°C). Bake 20 minutes. Remove lasagne from oven. Cut remaining mozzarella cheese into thin strips and arrange on lasagne. Bake 10 minutes longer. Let stand 10 minutes before cutting. Makes 6 to 8 servings.

Meat Sauce:

In a large skillet, brown beef and onion about 15 minutes, stirring to break up meat. Drain off excess fat. Stir in remaining ingredients. Cover and simmer 20 minutes or until slightly thickened, stirring occasionally. Makes about 4-1/2 cups.

Make an interesting sauce for pasta by heating 2 tablespoons of caraway or poppy seeds in butter until the butter begins to brown. Toss the sauce with 8 ounces of noodles, cooked and drained.

Pork Chops Aloha

Even if you use plain packaged noodles, you'll enjoy this casserole.

4 loin pork chops (1-1/2 inches thick)
1 tablespoon oil
1/2 cup water
Salt to taste
Freshly ground black pepper to taste
4 slices canned pineapple
4 thin orange slices
4 thin lemon slices
1/2 cup pineapple juice

1/2 cup orange juice
3 tablespoons honey
3 qts. water
1 tablespoon vegetable oil
Orange Pasta dough or Pineapple Pasta dough,
    page 14, cut in noodles, uncooked
1 to 2 tablespoons butter
1 tablespoon cold water
2 teaspoons cornstarch

Slash fat on pork chops at 1-inch intervals. Heat 1 tablespoon oil in a large skillet. Brown pork chops on both sides. Place pork chops in a shallow 2-quart baking dish. Add 1/2 cup water. Sprinkle each chop with salt to taste and pepper. Cover and place in cold oven. Set temperature control at 350°F (175°C). Bake 1 hour. Remove cover. Place a pineapple slice on each chop. Top each with an orange slice and a lemon slice. In a small bowl, mix pineapple juice, orange juice and honey. Pour juice over chops. Bake uncovered 30 minutes longer, basting occasionally with pan juices. Bring 3 quarts water to a rapid boil in a heavy 5-quart pot or Dutch oven. Add 1 tablespoon oil. Gradually add noodles, being sure water continues to boil. Cook noodles uncovered until tender but firm, stirring occasionally. Drain. Toss with 1 to 2 tablespoons butter. Remove pork chops from oven. Pour pan juices into a small saucepan. Mix 1 tablespoon cold water and cornstarch. Stir into sauce. Bring to a boil. Cook and stir until thickened. Pour over chops. Serve with buttered Orange or Pineapple Noodles. Makes 4 servings.

Here are a few terms you may find helpful when talking about pasta:
   Pasta fresca *is homemade or fresh pasta.* **Pasta secca** *is the packaged pasta you buy in the supermarket. And* **pasta verdi**, *or green pasta, has pureed spinach in the basic dough.*

Basque Chicken

Eggplant adds the unique taste to this classic dish.

1 (2-1/2-lb.) broiler-fryer chicken,
  cut in pieces
1 teaspoon salt
1/4 teaspoon black pepper
2 tablespoons olive oil
1 medium eggplant, peeled, cubed (4 cups)
1/2 lb. mushrooms, sliced
1/2 cup chopped onion
1 green pepper, cut in thin strips
1/2 cup cooked ham, cut in thin strips
1 large garlic clove, pressed

1 (15-oz.) can tomato sauce
1/3 cup dry white wine
1 cup water
1 chicken bouillon cube
1/2 teaspoon salt
1/8 teaspoon black pepper
2 qts. water
1-1/2 teaspoons salt
1 tablespoon vegetable oil
3/4 lb. mostaccioli, uncooked

Sprinkle chicken with 1 teaspoon salt and 1/4 teaspoon pepper. In a large skillet, heat olive oil. Brown chicken pieces on both sides until golden. Remove chicken and place in a 13" x 9" baking dish; reserve drippings in skillet. Sauté eggplant, mushrooms, onion, green pepper, ham and garlic in drippings until golden, about 5 minutes. Stir in tomato sauce, wine, 1 cup water, bouillon cube, 1/2 teaspoon salt and 1/8 teaspoon pepper. Bring to a boil. Pour over chicken. Cover and place in cold oven. Set temperature control at 350°F (175°C). Bake 50 minutes. Bring 2 quarts water to a rapid boil in a heavy 4-quart saucepan. Add 1-1/2 teaspoons salt and vegetable oil. Gradually add mostaccioli, being sure water continues to boil. Cook mostaccioli uncovered until tender but firm, stirring occasionally. Drain. Arrange cooked mostaccioli in baking dish around chicken pieces. Bake 5 minutes longer. Makes 4 servings.

Pasta that is not rinsed after cooking contains more B vitamins than pasta that has been rinsed.

Side Dishes

Pasta is one of the easiest foods to use as a side dish. Without even looking at a recipe in this section, you can select a nutritious vegetable pasta such as Broccoli Pasta or Onion Pasta, page 14, Raw Carrot Pasta, page 18, or Zucchini Pasta, page 15. Cook the pasta according to the directions on page 6. Then top it with butter and freshly grated Parmesan cheese and serve it with steaks, chops or a roast.

To make an easy butter and herb topping, mix 1/4 teaspoon each of dried leaf thyme, basil and oregano with 1/4 cup soft butter, then toss the butter with 8 ounces of drained cooked pasta. You can substitute 1/4 cup of thinly sliced green onions or 1 cup sliced mushrooms for the herbs and sauté them in the butter before adding to the pasta. Always serve grated Parmesan cheese or Romano cheese with these simple sauces.

For a quick and crunchy pasta, lightly brown 1/2 cup of slivered almonds in 1/4 cup of butter. Stir in 1 tablespoon of sesame seeds and toss the nut butter with the pasta.

For something a little out of the ordinary, serve Fried Soft Noodles. These are cooked noodles sautéed quickly in hot oil.

I use *orzo*, barley-like pasta that looks like rice, to make Stuffed Peppers and other stuffed vegetables. Orzo takes the place of traditional rice but it has a different texture and taste.

Menu
For Calorie Counters
Broiled Chicken
Sunflower Noodles, page 128
Lettuce Wedges With Lemon Dressing
Berries With Plain Yogurt
Coffee or Tea

Pasta & Fagioli

Kidney beans are added to the macaroni mixture in this Italian dish.

2 tablespoons olive oil
1 cup chopped onion
1 garlic clove, pressed
1 (1-lb.) can tomatoes, undrained, cut up
1 tablespoon minced fresh parsley
1 teaspoon salt
1/4 teaspoon black pepper
1/8 teaspoon dried rosemary, crushed
1 (15-oz.) can red or white kidney beans, undrained
1 cup elbow macaroni, uncooked (4 oz.)
Grated Romano or Parmesan cheese to taste

Heat oil in a large skillet. Sauté onion and garlic in oil until onion is golden. Add tomatoes with liquid, parsley, salt, pepper and rosemary. Bring to a boil. Reduce heat and simmer 5 minutes. Add beans with liquid and uncooked macaroni. Bring to a boil. Reduce heat and simmer 5 minutes longer until macaroni is tender but firm. Sprinkle with Romano or Parmesan cheese. Makes 4 servings.

Noodles Budapest

Crush the caraway seeds before adding them to the cabbage mixture.

10 cups water
2 teaspoons salt
1 tablespoon vegetable oil
8 cups medium noodles, uncooked (1 lb.)
1/4 cup vegetable oil
1 cup chopped onion
2 garlic cloves, pressed
1 lb. bacon

1 medium head cabbage, shredded
  (about 12 cups)
3 cups cottage cheese
1 cup dairy sour cream
1 teaspoon sugar
1/4 teaspoon black pepper
1/2 teaspoon caraway seeds, if desired

Bring water to a rapid boil in a heavy 5-quart pot or Dutch oven. Add salt and 1 tablespoon oil. Gradually add noodles, being sure water continues to boil. Cook noodles uncovered until tender but firm, stirring occasionally. Drain. Butter a 13" x 9" baking dish; set aside. Heat 1/4 cup oil in a heavy pot or Dutch oven. Sauté onion and garlic in oil until onion is golden. Add cooked noodles. Stir constantly over medium heat about 4 minutes. Remove noodle mixture from pot; set aside. Fry bacon in pot until crisp. Remove from pot. Cool bacon and crumble; set aside. Add shredded cabbage to bacon drippings. Cook and stir about 10 minutes until cabbage is wilted. Preheat oven to 350°F (175°C). In a large bowl, toss noodle mixture, wilted cabbage and half the crumbled bacon. In a medium bowl, mix cottage cheese, sour cream, sugar, pepper and caraway seeds, if desired. Pour cottage cheese mixture over noodle-cabbage mixture; toss to coat. Pour into prepared baking dish. Sprinkle with remaining crumbled bacon. Bake in preheated oven 20 minutes. Makes 6 to 8 servings.

Cottage Cheese Kugel

Served as a main dish, this Jewish casserole makes 4 servings.

1/2 cup butter or margarine
6 cups water
1 teaspoon salt
2 teaspoons vegetable oil
4 cups medium noodles, uncooked (8 oz.)

3 eggs
1 cup cottage cheese
1 cup dairy sour cream
1 teaspoon salt
1/8 teaspoon white pepper

Preheat oven to 350°F (175°C). Melt butter in an 11" x 7" baking dish; set aside. Bring water to a rapid boil in a heavy 3-quart saucepan. Add 1 teaspoon salt and oil. Gradually add noodles, being sure water continues to boil. Cook noodles uncovered until tender but firm, stirring occasionally. Drain. Beat eggs in a large bowl. Stir in cottage cheese, sour cream, 1 teaspoon salt and pepper. Spread butter over bottom of baking dish. Stir excess into cottage cheese mixture. Add cooked noodles; toss to coat. Spoon into prepared baking dish. Bake in preheated oven until golden, 45 minutes. May be served warm or cold. Makes 9 servings.

Sesame Noodles

Made with either egg noodles or plain noodles—the flavor and texture will still be delightful.

6 cups water
1 teaspoon salt
2 teaspoons vegetable oil
4 cups medium egg noodles, uncooked (8 oz.)

1/4 cup butter or margarine
2 tablespoons sesame seeds
1 cup chopped pimiento-stuffed olives
Freshly ground black pepper to taste

Bring water to a rapid boil in a heavy 3-quart saucepan. Add salt and oil. Gradually add noodles, being sure water continues to boil. Cook noodles uncovered until tender but firm, stirring occasionally. Drain. Melt butter or margarine in a large skillet. Add sesame seeds. Sauté until lightly browned. Add cooked noodles and olives. Toss lightly. Sprinkle with freshly ground black pepper. Serve immediately. Makes 6 servings.

Noodle Nests

Use these crisp nests as a base for creamed chicken, ham or seafood.

6 cups water
1 teaspoon salt

2 cups cluster vermicelli, uncooked (4 oz.)
Oil for deep-frying

Bring water to a rapid boil in a heavy 3-quart saucepan. Add salt. Gradually add vermicelli, being sure water continues to boil. Cook vermicelli uncovered until tender but firm, about 5 minutes, stirring occasionally. Drain. Oil six 3-1/2-inch miniature ring molds. Cut cooked vermicelli into 1/2-inch pieces. Press cooked vermicelli pieces 1/2 inch up all sides of each prepared mold. Refrigerate until firm, 1/2 hour. Heat oil to 365°F (185°C). At this temperature, a 1-inch cube of bread will turn golden brown in 50 seconds. Carefully remove noodles from ring mold. Fry in hot oil until golden, 3 to 4 minutes. If oil is too hot, rings will separate. Drain on paper towels. To reheat nests, preheat oven to 350°F (175°C). Bake nests until warm, 5 minutes. Makes 6 nests.

Fried Soft Noodles

If you make your own noodles, try Lemon Pasta, page 14.

6 cups water
1 teaspoon salt
2 teaspoons vegetable oil
4 cups medium noodles, uncooked (8 oz.)

2 tablespoons vegetable oil
1 cup chopped cooked asparagus or broccoli
1/3 cup grated Pecorino or Romano cheese
1 medium tomato, sliced, for garnish

Bring water to a rapid boil in a heavy 3-quart saucepan. Add salt and 2 teaspoons oil. Gradually add noodles, being sure water continues to boil. Cook noodles uncovered until tender but firm, stirring occasionally. Drain. Heat 2 tablespoons oil in a large skillet. Add cooked noodles and asparagus or broccoli. Sauté 4 minutes, stirring constantly. Spoon onto a warm platter. Sprinkle with cheese. Toss to coat. Place tomato slices on top. Serve immediately. Makes 4 to 6 servings.

Noodles Romanoff

Serve this rich and creamy meatless dish with cold corned beef.

6 cups water	2 cups creamed cottage cheese
1 teaspoon salt	2 cups dairy sour cream
2 teaspoons vegetable oil	1 tablespoon minced fresh parsley
4 cups noodles, uncooked (8 oz.)	1 tablespoon minced pimiento, drained
2 tablespoons butter	1/2 teaspoon salt
1/2 cup thinly sliced green onion	Tabasco sauce to taste
1 garlic clove, pressed	1/4 cup grated Romano cheese

Bring water to a rapid boil in a heavy 3-quart saucepan. Add 1 teaspoon salt and oil. Gradually add noodles, being sure water continues to boil. Cook noodles uncovered until tender but firm, stirring occasionally. Drain. Butter a 2-1/2-quart casserole; set aside. Preheat oven to 350°F (175°C). Melt butter in a small skillet. Sauté onion and garlic in butter. In a large bowl, beat cottage cheese and sour cream with a fork or whisk until blended. Stir in sautéed onion mixture, parsley, pimiento, 1/2 teaspoon salt, Tabasco sauce and cooked noodles. Spoon into prepared casserole. Top with grated Romano cheese. Bake in preheated oven 30 minutes. Makes 4 servings.

Variation

Substitute 3-1/2 cups low-fat cottage cheese for the 2 cups cottage cheese and 2 cups dairy sour cream.

Saucy Green Noodles

Highly nutritious yogurt becomes a tangy sauce.

6 tablespoons butter	1 teaspoon salt
1 tablespoon grated onion	2 teaspoons vegetable oil
2 tablespoons minced fresh parsley	4 cups green spinach noodles,
1 tablespoon snipped chives	uncooked (8 oz.)
1 teaspoon grated lemon peel	1/2 cup plain yogurt, room temperature
Garlic powder to taste	Grated Romano cheese for garnish
6 cups water	

In a small skillet, melt butter over medium heat. Sauté onion until golden. Add parsley, chives, lemon peel and garlic powder. Bring water to a rapid boil in a heavy 3-quart saucepan. Add salt and oil. Gradually add noodles, being sure water continues to boil. Cook noodles uncovered until tender but firm, stirring occasionally. Drain. Pour butter mixture over cooked noodles; toss gently to coat. Stir yogurt until creamy. Pour yogurt over cooked noodles; toss gently. Sprinkle with cheese. Serve immediately. Makes 6 to 8 servings.

Triple Cheese Bundt

Crunchy vegetable and raisins provide texture contrast.

10 cups water
2 teaspoons salt
1 tablespoon vegetable oil
4 cups elbow macaroni, uncooked (16 oz.)
4 eggs
3/4 cup half-and-half
1/2 cup milk
2 teaspoons salt
1/2 teaspoon white pepper
1/2 teaspoon mustard, Dijon-style

1/4 teaspoon Worcestershire sauce
1/2 cup chopped onion
3/4 cup raisins
1/2 cup chopped celery
1/2 cup chopped walnuts
1-1/2 cups grated American cheese (6 oz.)
1-1/2 cups grated Cheddar cheese (6 oz.)
1 cup grated fresh Parmesan cheese (4 oz.)
Mandarin orange sections for garnish

Bring water to a rapid boil in a heavy 5-quart pot or Dutch oven. Add 2 teaspoons salt and oil. Gradually add macaroni, being sure water continues to boil. Cook macaroni uncovered until tender but firm, stirring occasionally. Drain; keep warm. Butter and lightly flour a 12-cup Bundt pan; set aside. Preheat oven to 350°F (175°C). In a large bowl, beat eggs, half-and-half, milk, 2 teaspoons salt, white pepper, mustard and Worcestershire sauce. Add cooked macaroni, onion, raisins, celery, walnuts, American, Cheddar and Parmesan cheeses. Spoon into prepared pan. Bake 40 minutes in preheated oven. Cool 10 minutes. Loosen edges with a metal spatula. Place a platter upside-down over pan. Invert pan and platter. Remove pan. Garnish with orange sections. Serve immediately. Makes 10 to 12 servings.

Fettuccini With Brown Butter

So quick and easy you'll really enjoy this classic.

3 qts. water
1 tablespoon salt
1 tablespoon vegetable oil
1/2 lb. fettuccini, spaghetti or linguine,
  uncooked

4 tablespoons butter
Grated Parmesan cheese for garnish
Poppy seeds or sesame seeds for garnish

Bring water to a rapid boil in a heavy 5-quart pot or Dutch oven. Add salt and oil. Gradually add fettuccini, spaghetti or linguine, being sure water continues to boil. Cook pasta uncovered until tender but firm, stirring occasionally. Drain. Place in a warm serving bowl. Melt butter until frothy and brown. Pour over pasta immediately. Toss gently. Serve with grated Parmesan cheese and poppy seeds or sesame seeds. Makes 4 servings.

Variation

Substitute grated Romano or crumbled feta cheese for Parmesan cheese.

Fettuccini With Two Cheeses

Be sure the Gruyère cheese is marked aged natural. *Young cheeses tend to be stringy.*

4 tablespoons butter
2 tablespoons flour
2 cups milk
1/2 cup shredded Gruyère cheese (2 oz.)
1/2 cup shredded Gouda cheese (2 oz.)
1/3 cup golden raisins

5 qts. water
1 tablespoon salt
1 tablespoon vegetable oil
1 lb. fettuccini or spaghetti, uncooked
Grated Parmesan cheese

Melt butter in a medium saucepan. Stir in flour. Cook until bubbly. Gradually add milk, stirring constantly until thickened. Remove from heat. Stir in Gruyère and Gouda cheeses and raisins. Bring water to a rapid boil in a heavy 7-quart pot or Dutch oven. Add salt and oil. Gradually add fettuccini or spaghetti, being sure water continues to boil. Cook pasta uncovered until tender but firm, stirring occasionally. Drain. Spoon into a large warm serving bowl. Just before serving, heat sauce over medium heat until cheeses melt. Immediately pour sauce over pasta; toss gently. Sprinkle with grated Parmesan cheese. Makes 8 servings.

Spinach Noodles With Feta Cheese

To use dried mint in this Balkan dish, crush 1 teaspoon in the palm of your hand.

6 cups water
1 teaspoon salt
2 teaspoons vegetable oil
4 cups green spinach egg noodles,
    uncooked (8 oz.)
1/2 cup minced onion
1 tablespoon olive oil
1 (10-oz.) pkg. frozen spinach, thawed,
    drained, chopped

4 oz. feta cheese, crumbled
2 eggs
1/2 cup half-and-half
1/2 cup cottage cheese
1/2 teaspoon salt
1/8 teaspoon black pepper
1/8 teaspoon garlic powder
2 teaspoons chopped fresh mint leaves,
    if desired

Bring water to a rapid boil in a heavy 3-quart saucepan. Add 1 teaspoon salt and vegetable oil. Gradually add noodles, being sure water continues to boil. Cook noodles uncovered until tender but firm, stirring occasionally. Drain; set aside. Butter a 9-inch square baking dish; set aside. In a small skillet, sauté onion in olive oil until golden. In a large bowl, mix cooked noodles, spinach, sautéed onion and feta cheese. Beat eggs in a small bowl. Stir in half-and-half, cottage cheese, 1/2 teaspoon salt, pepper, garlic powder and mint leaves, if desired. Pour over noodle mixture. Mix well. Spoon into prepared baking dish. Place in cold oven. Set temperature control at 350°F (175°C). Bake 45 minutes. Remove from oven. Let stand 5 minutes before cutting. Makes 9 servings.

Velvety Vermicelli With Potato

As soon as you turn on the oven, set the timer for the recommended baking time.

4 cups water
1/2 teaspoon salt
1 teaspoon vegetable oil
1-1/4 cups broken vermicelli, uncooked (2 oz.)
1 (1-1/4-oz.) pkg. cheese sauce mix
1 cup milk
1/4 teaspoon curry powder

1 medium boiling potato, peeled, cooked, diced
1 (10-oz.) pkg. frozen brussels sprouts, cooked, drained
1 green onion, thinly sliced
1 tablespoon chopped pimiento, drained

Butter a 1-quart casserole; set aside. Bring 4 cups water to a rapid boil in a heavy 2-quart saucepan. Add salt and oil. Gradually add vermicelli, being sure water continues to boil. Cook vermicelli uncovered until tender but firm, stirring occasionally. Drain. Prepare cheese sauce mix with milk following package directions. Stir in curry powder. In a large bowl, toss together potato, brussels sprouts, cooked vermicelli, onion, pimiento and cheese sauce. Pour into prepared casserole. Place in cold oven. Set temperature control at 350°F (175°C). Bake until sauce bubbles, 20 minutes. Serve immediately. Makes 4 servings.

Mostaccioli à la Crème

Consider using Edam, Swiss or brick cheese in place of Parmesan cheese in this beautiful buffet dish.

4 qts. water
1 tablespoon salt
1 lb. mostaccioli, uncooked
4 cups milk

1 cup whipping cream
1/4 lb. butter (8 tablespoons)
1-1/4 cups grated Parmesan cheese
Salt and pepper to taste

Bring water to a rapid boil in a large pot. Add 1 tablespoon salt and mostaccioli. Cook only half the time called for in the package directions. Drain. In a large heavy 6-quart pot or Dutch oven, combine milk and whipping cream. Remove 1 cup milk-cream mixture from the pot; set aside. Add mostaccioli to mixture in pot. Cook over medium heat until all liquid is absorbed or mostaccioli is tender but firm. Thinly slice 4 tablespoons butter into the bottom of a 13" x 9" baking dish. Sprinkle 1/2 cup cheese over butter. Spoon half the cooked mostaccioli mixture over cheese. Sprinkle with another 1/2 cup of cheese. Top with remaining mostaccioli mixture. Sprinkle with salt and pepper to taste. Pour the reserved 1 cup milk-cream mixture over mostaccioli mixture. Sprinkle with remaining 1/4 cup cheese. Thinly slice remaining 4 tablespoons butter over cheese. Place in cold oven. Set temperature control at 350°F (175°C). Bake until golden, 30 minutes. Let stand 10 minutes before cutting. Makes 12 servings.

Pimiento Noodle Ring

Fill the noodle ring with your favorite creamed meat or vegetable.

2 cups water
1/2 teaspoon salt
1 cup broken medium egg noodles,
   uncooked (2 oz.)
6 egg yolks
1-1/2 cups hot milk
1-1/2 cups grated American or
   Monterey Jack cheese (6 oz.)

1 cup soft breadcrumbs
1/4 cup butter, melted
1 small canned pimiento, chopped
1/4 cup chopped green pepper
3/4 teaspoon salt
1/8 teaspon white pepper
1/8 teaspoon onion salt
Paprika for garnish

Generously butter a 5-cup ring mold; set aside. Bring water to a rapid boil in a heavy 2-quart saucepan. Add 1/2 teaspoon salt. Gradually add noodles, being sure water continues to boil. Cook noodles uncovered until tender but firm, stirring occasionally. Drain. Preheat oven to 350°F (175°C). In a large bowl, beat egg yolks. Stir in hot milk and cheese. Add cooked noodles, breadcrumbs, butter, pimiento or sweet red pepper, green pepper, 3/4 teaspoon salt, white pepper and onion salt. Pour into prepared ring mold. Place ring mold in a large pan of hot water. Place pan with ring mold in oven. Bake in preheated oven until a knife inserted off center comes out clean, 50 minutes. Let stand 10 minutes. Loosen sides of mold with the blade of a metal spatula. Place a platter upside-down over mold. Invert mold and platter. Remove mold. Sprinkle noodle ring with paprika. Fill with hot creamed meat or vegetables. Makes 6 to 8 servings.

Sunflower Noodles

If fresh bean sprouts are not available, use canned sliced water chestnuts.

6 cups water
1 teaspoon salt
2 teaspoons vegetable oil
4 cups medium noodles, uncooked (8 oz.)
1/4 cup butter
1 teaspoon salt

1/8 teaspoon black pepper
1/2 cup sunflower seeds
1/4 cup sesame seeds
1/2 cup fresh bean sprouts
1/4 cup chopped cucumber
Avocado slices for garnish

Bring water to a rapid boil in a heavy 3-quart saucepan. Add 1 teaspoon salt and oil. Gradually add noodles, being sure water continues to boil. Cook noodles uncovered until tender but firm, stirring occasionally. Drain. Melt butter in a small skillet. Add 1 teaspoon salt, pepper, sunflower seeds and sesame seeds. Sauté until sesame seeds are golden. Place hot cooked noodles in a warm serving bowl. Spoon sesame seed mixture over noodles. Add bean sprouts and cucumber. Toss gently to coat. Garnish with avocado slices. Serve immediately. Makes 4 servings.

1/Pour pimiento noodle mixture into a well-buttered ring mold. Place in a pan of hot water to bake.

How To Make Pimiento Noodle Ring

2/After baking noodles, let mold sit for 10 minutes before unmolding. To loosen sides, run a metal spatula round the edge of the mold. Invert onto a platter and remove mold.

3/Fill center with vegetables or hot creamed meat or fish. Garnish with your prettiest vegetables.

Stuffed Peppers

Crown pepper halves with tomato slices before baking.

1/4 cup vegetable oil	1/2 cup chopped fresh parsley
1 medium onion, chopped	2 small tomatoes, peeled
1 cup orzo	1/4 cup tomato sauce
1 teaspoon salt	1-1/2 cups water
1/4 teaspoon black pepper	2 tablespoons tomato sauce
1 teaspoon dried dill weed	3 large green peppers

Grease a 9-inch baking dish; set aside. Heat oil in a large skillet over medium heat. Sauté onion until golden. Stir in orzo, salt, pepper, dill and parsley. Simmer 2 minutes, stirring occasionally. Dice 1 tomato. Add diced tomato, 1/4 cup tomato sauce and 1 cup water to orzo mixture. Bring to a boil. Reduce heat and simmer until water is absorbed, 10 minutes. Cut peppers in half lengthwise. Remove seeds and membranes. Fill pepper halves with orzo mixture. Place in prepared baking dish. In a small bowl, combine remaining 1/2 cup water and 2 tablespoons tomato sauce. Pour around peppers in baking dish. Cut remaining tomato into thin slices. Arrange on top of peppers. Cover and place in cold oven. Set temperature control at 350°F (175°C). Bake 1 hour. Serve immediately. Makes 6 servings.

Hot Onion Pie

Whole-Wheat Pasta, page 15, is delicious with onions. Use only a third of the dough.

4 cups water	1 teaspoon seasoning salt
1/2 teaspoon salt	4 cups thinly sliced onions
1 teaspoon vegetable oil	1 egg
2 cups thin noodles, uncooked (4 oz.)	1/2 cup dairy sour cream
4 tablespoons butter	1/2 cup shredded Swiss cheese (2 oz.)
2 tablespoons water	1/8 teaspoon salt
1 tablespoon Worcestershire sauce	Freshly ground black pepper to taste

Bring 4 cups water to a rapid boil in a heavy 2-quart saucepan. Add 1/2 teaspoon salt and oil. Gradually add noodles, being sure water continues to boil. Cook noodles uncovered until tender but firm, stirring occasionally. Drain; set aside. In a 10-inch skillet, combine butter, 2 tablespoons water, Worcestershire sauce, seasoning salt and onions. Cover and cook over medium heat until onions are tender, stirring occasionally. Remove onion mixture from skillet; set aside. Beat egg in a medium bowl. Blend in sour cream, Swiss cheese, 1/8 teaspoon salt and pepper. Add cooked noodles; toss to coat. Spread noodle mixture in bottom of skillet. Spoon onion mixture over noodle mixture. Cover and cook over medium heat 15 to 20 minutes. Serve hot. Makes 8 to 10 servings.

Rotini With Green Beans

Colorful and spicy, this dish with twisted macaroni goes well with pork or lamb chops.

1/2 cup chopped onion
1 cup minced celery
4 tablespoons olive oil
1 (16-oz.) can tomato bits
1 (4-oz.) can mushrooms, drained
1/4 cup dry white wine
1/4 cup minced fresh parsley
1/2 teaspoon salt
1/4 teaspoon dried oregano
1/4 teaspoon dried thyme

1/8 teaspoon black pepper
2 (9-oz.) pkgs. frozen green beans or
   mixed vegetables, cooked, drained
1 (4-oz.) can water chestnuts, drained,
   thinly sliced
6 cups water
1 teaspoon salt
1 tablespoon vegetable oil
2 cups rotini or tortellini, uncooked (8 oz.)
1 cup shredded mozzarella cheese (4 oz.)

Butter a 2-quart casserole; set aside. In a medium saucepan, sauté onion and celery in olive oil until golden. Stir in tomato bits, mushrooms, wine, parsley, 1/2 teaspoon salt, oregano, thyme and pepper. Cover and simmer 10 minutes. Add green beans or mixed vegetables. Cover and cook 5 minutes longer. Stir in water chestnuts. Bring water to a rapid boil in a heavy 3-quart saucepan. Add 1 teaspoon salt and vegetable oil. Gradually add rotini or tortellini, being sure water continues to boil. Cook pasta uncovered until tender but firm, stirring occasionally. Drain. Arrange pasta in bottom of prepared casserole. Sprinkle with mozzarella cheese. Spread with green bean or mixed vegetable mixture. Cover and place in cold oven. Set temperature control at 350°F (175°C). Bake 15 minutes. Serve immediately. Makes 6 to 8 servings.

Fettuccini Alfredo

It's too easy to be so good!

3 qts. water
1 tablespoon salt
1 tablespoon vegetable oil
1/2 lb. fettuccini, uncooked
1/4 cup butter

1/2 cup half-and-half or whipping cream
1/2 cup grated fresh Parmesan cheese (2 oz.)
Freshly ground black pepper to taste
Freshly grated nutmeg for garnish

Bring water to a rapid boil in a heavy 5-quart pot or Dutch oven. Add salt and oil. Gradually add fettuccini, being sure water continues to boil. Cook fettuccini uncovered until tender but firm, stirring occasionally. Drain. In a medium saucepan or chafing dish, melt butter with 1/4 cup half-and-half or cream. Simmer 1 minute to thicken. Remove from heat. Add cooked fettuccini to butter mixture. Toss gently to coat. Add remaining 1/4 cup half-and-half or cream, Parmesan cheese and pepper; gently toss. Serve in a chafing dish or large serving dish. Sprinkle with nutmeg. Makes 4 servings.

Yogurt-Topped Vegetable Casserole

Hearty enough to serve four people as a main dish.

2 qts. water
1-1/2 teaspoons salt
1 tablespoon vegetable oil
2-1/2 cups mostaccioli or thick macaroni,
   broken in quarters, uncooked
1 medium eggplant (about 1 lb.)
1 teaspoon salt

1/2 cup vegetable oil
1 lb. zucchini, cut lengthwise into
   1/8-inch slices
1 egg
1/4 cup milk
2 tablespoons grated Parmesan cheese
Yogurt Topping, see below

Yogurt Topping:
1 cup plain yogurt, room temperature
1 egg, slightly beaten

1 teaspoon cornstarch
1 tablespoon water

Bring water to a rapid boil in a heavy 4-quart saucepan. Add 1-1/2 teaspoons salt and oil. Gradually add mostaccioli or macaroni, being sure water continues to boil. Cook pasta uncovered until tender but firm, stirring occasionally. Drain. Generously butter an 11" x 7" baking dish and oil a baking sheet; set both aside. Peel eggplant lengthwise, leaving on some strips of peel. Slice crosswise 1/8 inch thick. Sprinkle with 1 teaspoon salt. Drain in a colander 20 minutes. Rinse off salt under cold water; lightly squeeze slices to remove excess water. Place on prepared baking sheet. Drizzle 1/4 cup oil over eggplant slices. Broil 4 inches from heat until golden brown, 10 minutes on each side. Remove eggplant slices. Place zucchini on baking sheet. Drizzle with remaining 1/4 cup oil. Broil 4 inches from heat until golden brown, 10 minutes on each side. Remove zucchini slices. Preheat oven to 350°F (175°C). Beat eggs in a small bowl. Stir in milk. Pour over cooked macaroni or mostaccioli. Mix well. In prepared baking dish, layer macaroni mixture, eggplant slices, 1 tablespoon Parmesan cheese and zucchini slices. Prepare Yogurt Topping. Spoon topping over casserole. Sprinkle with remaining Parmesan cheese. Bake until glaze is set, 20 minutes. Makes 8 servings.

Yogurt Topping:
Stir yogurt until creamy. Mix in egg, cornstarch and water to blend.

Top baked casseroles with sautéed green pepper rings, minced parsley, paprika, sliced pimiento-stuffed olives or sliced green onions.

Deutsch Meatballs With Spaetzle

Shaking the skillet prevents the meatballs from sticking.

Deutsch Meatballs, see below
2 tablespoons vegetable oil
1 (10-1/2-oz.) can beef broth
1 (4-oz.) can mushroom stems and pieces
1/2 cup chopped onion

1/2 teaspoon caraway seeds
Bavarian Spaetzle, page 17
1 cup dairy sour cream
1 tablespoon all-purpose flour

Deutsch Meatballs:
1 lb. lean ground beef
1/4 cup fine dry breadcrumbs
1/4 cup milk
1 egg, slightly beaten

1 tablespoon minced fresh parsley
1 teaspoon salt
1/4 teaspoon poultry seasoning
Black pepper to taste

Prepare Deutsch Meatballs. Heat oil in a large skillet. Brown meatballs on all sides, shaking skillet frequently. Add broth, mushroom stems and pieces, onion and caraway seeds. Bring to a boil. Reduce heat. Cover and simmer 30 minutes. Prepare Bavarian Spaetzle. Blend sour cream and flour. Gradually stir into broth and meatball mixture. Stir constantly over low heat until mixture thickens but do not boil. Serve immediately with Bavarian Spaetzle. Makes 5 or 6 servings.

Deutsch Meatballs:

In a medium bowl, lightly mix all ingredients. Shape into twenty-four 1-1/2-inch meatballs.

To give plain noodles a delightful flavor, try this: Cook 4 cups of noodles (8 ounces) in 4 cups of orange juice and 4 cups of water with 1 teaspoon of salt and 1 teaspoon of oil; drain. Stir 1 tablespoon of grated orange peel into 1/4 cup of melting butter. Pour the butter mixture over the noodles; toss well.

Sauces

Like potatoes and rice, pasta soaks up sauce. How much sauce depends on how thick or thin the pasta is. As a general rule, thin sauces taste best with thin forms of pasta and thicker sauces go well with the thicker varieties.

One of the joys of pasta is it cooks fast. Prepare the sauce, set it aside and then cook the pasta. The sauce can be reheated before serving.

Strong cheeses such as Parmesan add zest to pasta. Do grate your own cheese—the quality is usually much better. Cheese may be grated just before serving or, if you prefer, place small individual hand graters at each place setting.

Whenever you prepare a long-cooking sauce such as Classic Tomato Sauce, make large quantities. Pour the sauce into 1-pint large-mouth containers and freeze it. Allow 1 inch in the top of the container for expansion. Use the frozen sauce within 3 months.

Creamy Crab Sauce, Red Clam Sauce, White Clam Sauce and Red Tuna Sauce are in Fish & Seafood, pages 96 to 104.

Menu
Pasta Pronto
Broccoli-Cheese Cornucopias, page 52
Cheddar Cheese Sauce, below
Bibb Lettuce With Hearts of Palm
Garlic & Oil Dressing, page 42
Toated Buttered French Rolls
Fresh Fruit and Wine Compote
Coffee

Cheddar Cheese Sauce

For a sensational color contrast, serve this sauce over Beet Pasta, page 14.

2 tablespoons butter
2 tablespoons flour
1-1/4 cups cold milk

1/2 teaspoon salt
White pepper to taste
3/4 cup grated Cheddar cheese (3 oz.)

In a 1-quart saucepan, melt butter over low heat. Stir in flour. Continue stirring until bubbly. Stir in milk, salt and pepper. Continue stirring over medium heat until thick and smooth, about 8 minutes. Add cheese; stir over low heat to melt cheese. Makes about 2 cups.

Serving Suggestions: Pour sauce over hot cooked noodles made with Broccoli Pasta, page 14 or Spinach Pasta, page 15. Serve with a crisp salad.

Green Pepper Sauce

Minced green pepper in a creamy sauce gives a slightly pungent flavor.

4 tablespoons butter
1 cup green pepper, minced
4 tablespoons all-purpose flour, sifted
1/2 teaspoon salt

Black pepper to taste
2 cups milk
1/2 cup finely shredded Cheddar cheese
  (2 oz.)

Melt butter in a 1-quart saucepan. Add green pepper. Sauté until pepper is golden. Stir in flour, salt and pepper. Add milk. Stir constantly over medium heat until sauce thickens. Reduce heat. Add cheese; stir until melted. Makes about 2 cups.

Serving Suggestions: Spoon sauce over hot cooked noodles made with Egg Noodle Pasta, page 15, or Zucchini Pasta, page 14.

Herb Sauce

You probably have these ingredients on hand right now!

4 tablespoons butter
1/2 cup chopped onion
1 garlic clove, pressed
1 cup chopped, peeled tomatoes

2 tablespoons water
1/2 teaspoon dried oregano
1/2 teaspoon Italian herbs
1/8 teaspoon salt

Melt butter in a small saucepan over medium heat. Sauté onion and garlic until onion is golden. Stir in tomatoes, water, oregano, Italian herbs and salt. Bring to a boil. Cover and simmer about 15 minutes. Makes 1 cup.

Serving Suggestions: Spoon sauce over hot cooked noodles made with Whole-Wheat Pasta, page 15, Egg Noodle Pasta or Plain Pasta, page 14.

Bavarian Beer Sauce

When you serve broiled pork chops or steak, top Spaetzle, page 16, with this tasty sauce.

2 tablespoons butter
2 tablespoons flour
1 cup bottled barbecue sauce with onions

1 (12-oz.) bottle beer
1/3 cup ketchup

Melt butter over medium heat, in a medium saucepan. Stir in flour. Continue stirring until bubbly. Stir in barbecue sauce, beer and ketchup. Stir constantly until thickened. Makes about 2 cups sauce.

Serving Suggestions: Spoon sauce over hot cooked wide noodles made with Zucchini Pasta, page 15, or Spaetzle, page 16. Sprinkle with grated Parmesan cheese if desired.

Broccoli Sauce

Make only what you can serve immediately; this sauce cannot be frozen or stored.

1/4 cup water
1/4 teaspoon salt
1/2 (10-oz.) pkg. frozen chopped broccoli,
 (1 cup)
2 tablespoons butter

2 teaspoons cornstarch
1 tablespoon water
1 cup whipping cream
Freshly ground pepper to taste

Bring 1/4 cup water to a boil in a 1-quart saucepan. Add salt and frozen chopped broccoli. Cook broccoli in salted water according to package directions. Drain. Press to remove as much water from broccoli as possible. Add butter to broccoli; sauté about 1 minute. Blend cornstarch with 1 tablespoon water. Stir into broccoli and butter. Add whipping cream and pepper to broccoli mixture. Stir constantly over medium heat until slightly thickened. Makes about 1-1/4 cups.

Serving Suggestions: Serve sauce over hot cooked noodles made with Onion Pasta, page 14, or Whole-Wheat Pasta, page 15. Sprinkle with grated sharp Cheddar cheese and 1 small peeled tomato, seeded, chopped.

Zucchini Sauce Supreme

Delicate cream sauce adds gourmet appeal to pasta.

2 tablespoons butter
1-1/2 cups grated raw zucchini
1 tablespoon grated onion
1/3 cup half-and-half

1/8 teaspoon dried dill weed
1/8 teaspoon garlic salt
Black pepper to taste
1/2 cup dairy sour cream

Melt butter in a medium skillet. Sauté zucchini and onion in butter over medium heat until golden. Add half-and-half, dill weed, garlic salt and pepper. Stir constantly over low heat about 1 minute. Stir in sour cream. Heat to serving temperature. Makes about 1 cup sauce.

Serving Suggestions: Spoon sauce over hot cooked noodles made with Egg Noodle Pasta, page 14, Semolina Flour Pasta or Zucchini Pasta, page 15. Garnish with lengthwise grated carrot.

If you reheat a cheese sauce in a double boiler, it will not scorch.

Bolognese Meat Sauce

Just a touch of cloves and nutmeg enhances the flavor.

1 tablespoon vegetable oil	1 (16-oz.) can tomatoes, chopped
1 lb. lean ground beef	1 cup beef broth
1/3 cup chopped onion	2 tablespoons tomato paste
1/3 cup chopped celery	1 teaspoon salt
1/4 cup grated carrot	1/4 teaspoon black pepper
2 tablespoons pine nuts	Cloves to taste
4 slices ham, cut in julienne strips	Nutmeg to taste
1/4 cup dry sherry wine	

Heat oil in a large skillet, over medium heat. Sauté beef and onion, stirring to break up meat. Add celery, carrot and pine nuts. Sauté until meat is browned. Stir in ham strips and wine. Cook until liquid has evaporated. Stir in remaining ingredients. Bring to a boil. Cover and simmer about 1 hour. Makes about 3-1/2 cups.

Serving Suggestions: Spoon over hot cooked noodles made with Plain Pasta, page 14, or Whole-Wheat Pasta, page 15. Sprinkle with Parmesan cheese.

How To Make Bolognese Meat Sauce

1/Sauté meat with vegetables before mixing in ham strips. Add the tomatoes and broth to the meat mixture.

2/Simmer tomatoes, broth and meat mixture for 1 hour to thicken the sauce. Spoon over hot cooked noodles.

Classic Tomato Sauce

Use this tasty sauce instead of your usual lasagne sauce.

2 garlic cloves, pressed
1 tablespoon olive oil
1 (8-oz.) can tomato sauce
1 (6-oz.) can tomato paste
1-1/2 cups water
1 cup peeled and diced fresh tomatoes or
   1 cup diced canned tomatoes
2 tablespoons butter
1 tablespoon Parmesan cheese

1 teaspoon sugar
1/2 teaspoon salt
2 teaspoons dried oregano
1/2 teaspoon dried basil
1/8 teaspoon black pepper
1/8 teaspoon dried thyme
1/8 teaspoon celery salt
1/8 teaspoon dried tarragon

In a large skillet, sauté garlic in olive oil until golden. Add remaining ingredients. Mix well; bring to a boil. Cover and simmer about 1 hour. Makes about 3-1/2 cups sauce.

Serving Suggestions: Spoon sauce over hot cooked noodles made from Plain Pasta, page 14, Whole-Wheat Pasta or Semolina Flour Pasta, page 15. Sprinkle with grated Parmesan cheese.

Fresh Tomato Sauce

A refreshing, light, uncooked sauce.

1/3 cup olive oil
3 large ripe tomatoes, peeled, cubed
1/2 cup chopped fresh parsley leaves
2 tablespoons minced celery leaves

1 garlic clove, pressed
1 teaspoon salt
1/4 teaspoon freshly ground black pepper

In a medium bowl, combine all ingredients. Mix well. Makes about 2-1/2 cups.

Variation

Add any one or a combination of the following: 1 green onion, thinly sliced, 1/4 cup chopped green pepper, 1/4 cup chopped black olives, 1/2 cup thinly sliced fresh mushrooms or 1/2 cup chopped cooked shrimp or crab.

Serving Suggestions: Toss sauce with 1 pound hot cooked linguine, fettuccini, fusilli or spaghetti. Sprinkle with Parmesan cheese.

To thin down thick red sauce for pasta, add a little brown stock or red wine. To thin a white sauce, stir in a little milk, cream or white wine.

Ratatouille Sauce

Your own garden vegetables make this refreshing sauce.

1 large eggplant, peeled (about 2 lbs.)
1/2 cup vegetable oil
3 medium zucchini, sliced (about 1 lb.)
1/2 cup chopped onion

2 whole medium tomatoes, peeled, cubed
1/2 cup tomato sauce
1 teaspoon salt
1/8 teaspoon black pepper

Cut eggplant into 3/4-inch cubes. Heat oil in a large skillet over medium heat. Add cubed eggplant, zucchini and onion. Sauté until lightly browned, about 7 minutes, stirring often. Add tomatoes, tomato sauce, salt and pepper. Cover and simmer about 5 minutes.

Serving Suggestions: Spoon sauce over hot cooked noodles made from Broccoli Pasta, page 14, Zucchini Pasta or Spinach Pasta, page 15. Garnish with parsley sprigs and grated cheese.

Mushroom Meat Sauce

Add 1 cup tomato juice for a thinner sauce.

1 lb. lean ground beef
1 lb. fresh mushrooms, sliced
2 tablespoons chopped onion
1 garlic clove, pressed
1 (15-oz.) can tomato sauce with bits
1 (10-1/2-oz.) can tomato puree
1 cup water

2 beef bouillon cubes
1 tablespoon grated Parmesan cheese
1 teaspoon dried oregano
1 teaspoon sugar
1/2 teaspoon dried basil
1/8 teaspoon black pepper

In a large skillet, brown meat, mushrooms, onion and garlic. Stir in tomato sauce, tomato puree, water, bouillon cubes, Parmesan cheese, oregano, sugar, basil and pepper. Stir to blend all ingredients. Bring to a boil. Cover and reduce heat. Simmer 30 minutes. Makes about 4 cups.

Serving Suggestions: Serve sauce over hot cooked noodles made from Plain Pasta or Egg Pasta, page 14. This would also be a nice sauce to use for lasagne.

Pronto Parsley Sauce

You'll make this quick sauce often to top pasta or vegetables.

1 (10-3/4-oz.) can cream of celery soup
1/2 cup milk

2 tablespoons minced fresh parsley
1 teaspoon celery seeds

Combine soup and milk in a small saucepan. Cook over medium heat until mixture comes to a boil. Remove from heat. Stir in parsley and celery seeds. Makes about 1-3/4 cups.

Serving Suggestions: Pour sauce over hot cooked noodles made from Raw Carrot Pasta, page 18.

Spinach Pesto Sauce

To make authentic pesto sauce, omit the spinach and dried basil and add 2 cups of fresh basil leaves.

3/4 cup olive oil
2 cups packed fresh spinach leaves, washed,
    drained, stems removed, coarsely chopped
1/2 cup chopped fresh parsley
1/2 cup grated Parmesan cheese

1 small garlic clove, cut in half
1 teaspoon dried basil
1/2 teaspoon salt
Black pepper to taste
2 tablespoons pine nuts, if desired

Place oil, spinach, parsley, Parmesan cheese, garlic, basil, salt, pepper and pine nuts, if desired, in blender or food processor container. Cover and blend or process about 45 seconds. If sauce is too thick, stir in 1 to 2 teaspoons hot water. Makes about 1-1/2 cups.

Serving Suggestions: Toss sauce with hot cooked noodles made with Semolina Flour Pasta, page 15, or Plain Pasta, page 14.

Cauliflower Sauce

Cauliflower should be cooked until tender but firm.

1 teaspoon butter
1/4 cup chopped walnuts
2 tablespoons butter
1 tablespoon all-purpose flour
1 cup half-and-half
2/3 cup milk

1 cup diced raw cauliflower
1/4 teaspoon salt
White pepper to taste
1/2 cup grated Swiss cheese (2 oz.)
1/3 cup dry white wine

Melt 1 teaspoon butter in a medium saucepan. Sauté walnuts 3 minutes; set aside. Melt additional 2 tablespoons butter in pan. Blend flour into butter. Simmer until bubbly. Slowly stir in half-and-half and milk. Cook until smooth and slightly thickened, stirring constantly. Add cauliflower. Cook 1 minute. Add salt, pepper and cheese. Stir gently to melt cheese. Add wine and sautéed nuts. Heat to serving temperature but do not boil. Makes 2 cups.

Serving Suggestions: Serve sauce over hot cooked noodles made with Spinach Pasta, page 15, linguine, mostaccioli or fettuccini. Garnish with freshly grated nutmeg, if desired.

To substitute cornstarch for flour when thickening a sauce, use 1-1/2 teaspoons cornstarch for each tablespoon of flour.

Parsley Sauce

This piquant sauce over noodles is delicious with fried perch, sole or red snapper.

1 tablespoon instant minced onion
1 tablespoon water
1/4 cup vegetable oil
1 tablespoon plus 1 teaspoon lemon juice
1/4 cup minced fresh parsley

1 teaspoon dried oregano
1/2 teaspoon dried dill weed
1/4 teaspoon salt
1/8 teaspoon black pepper

In a small bowl, sprinkle onion in water. Let stand a few minutes to plump onion. In another small bowl, beat 1/4 cup oil while slowly adding lemon juice. Stir in parsley, oregano, dill, salt, pepper and plumped onion. Makes about 1/2 cup.

Serving Suggestions: Spoon sauce over hot cooked noodles made with Plain Pasta, page 14, or Spaetzle, page 16. Garnish with grated Romano cheese. Especially good served with seafood.

Whipping Cream Sauce

A delicious uncooked sauce that is rich and creamy.

2 oz. cream cheese, room temperature
1/2 cup whipping cream
1 cup milk

1 tablespoon snipped chives
1 tablespoon minced fresh parsley

In a small bowl, stir cream cheese. Blend in whipping cream, milk, chives and parsley. Makes about 2 cups sauce.

Variation

When noodles are made with Egg Pasta, page 14, add 1/4 teaspoon garlic salt and a dash of freshly ground pepper to the sauce. Garnish with grated Parmesan cheese.

Serving Suggestions: Spoon sauce over hot cooked noodles made with Raw Carrot Pasta, page 18, Orange Pasta or Pineapple Pasta, page 14. If using orange or pineapple noodles omit chives and parsley.

One (8-ounce) can of tomato sauce can be substituted for 1 cup of tomato puree. One (6-ounce) can of tomato paste mixed with 1 cup of water can be substituted for 2 (8-ounce) cans of tomato sauce.

Neapolitan Sauce

If you want a thicker sauce, simmer 1/2 hour longer.

6 slices bacon
1/2 cup chopped onion
1/2 cup chopped celery
1/4 cup minced carrot
2 slices ham, chopped
3 tablespoons dry red wine
1 (16-oz.) can tomatoes, chopped

1 cup beef broth
2 tablespoons minced fresh parsley
1 teaspoon salt
1 teaspoon dried oregano
1/4 teaspoon dried basil
1/4 teaspoon black pepper

In a large skillet, cook bacon until crisp. Set bacon aside to cool, then crumble. Add onion, celery, carrot and ham to bacon drippings. Sauté over medium-low heat until onion is golden. Add wine; simmer until liquid has evaporated. Stir in crumbled bacon, tomatoes, broth, parsley, salt, oregano, basil and pepper. Bring to a boil. Cover and reduce heat. Simmer 1 hour. Makes about 4 cups.

Serving Suggestions: Spoon sauce over hot cooked noodles made from Zucchini Pasta, page 15, or 1 pound of spaghetti. Sprinkle with Parmesan cheese.

Mediterranean Sauce

Hearty sausage and zucchini sauce over hot pasta is a satisfying dish.

1 lb. bulk Italian sausage
1-1/2 lbs. zucchini, sliced (about 6 cups)
3 tablespoons all-purpose flour
1/3 cup chopped onion
2 tomatoes, peeled, cubed

1/4 teaspoon salt
1/8 teaspoon black pepper
2-1/2 cups milk
1/2 cup chablis wine
2 teaspoons grated Parmesan cheese

In a large skillet, break sausage into small pieces. Cook until golden brown. Coat zucchini with flour. Add zucchini and onion to cooked sausage. Sauté until zucchini is golden brown, about 5 minutes. Add tomatoes, salt and pepper. Cover and cook 5 minutes. Stir in milk and wine. Continue cooking until thick and bubbly. Remove from heat. Stir in cheese. Makes about 4 cups.

Variation

Substitute 1-1/2 lbs. eggplant, cut in 3/4-inch cubes for zucchini. To prepare eggplant, place in a colander. Sprinkle with 1 teaspoon salt; let stand 20 minutes. Rinse with a little cold water; squeeze lightly to remove excess water. Coat with flour; sauté until golden brown.

Serving Suggestions: Spoon sauce over hot cooked noodles made with Egg Pasta, page 14, Semolina Flour Pasta or Zucchini Pasta, page 15. Garnish with sprigs of fresh parsley.

Toasted Almond Sauce

A delightful crunchy taste.

4 tablespoons butter
2 tablespoons flour
2 cups half-and-half

1/4 teaspoon salt
1/2 cup thinly sliced brick cheese (2 oz.)
1/2 cup toasted slivered almonds

In a small saucepan, melt butter over medium heat. Stir in flour. Cook until bubbly. Slowly blend in half-and-half and salt, stirring until thickened. Remove from heat. Stir cheese and almonds into sauce until cheese melts. Makes about 2 cups sauce.

Serving Suggestions: Prepare Sweet Dessert Manicotti, page 20, or Pineapple Pasta, page 14. If using Sweet Dessert Manicotti, fill cooked pasta with applesauce and spoon Toasted Almond Sauce over the top. If using Pineapple Pasta, cut in wide noodles. Toss cooked pasta with Toasted Almond Sauce.

Tangy Tomato Sauce

Leave out the carrots if you want to puree this sauce in your blender.

3 tablespoons olive oil
1 tablespoon butter
1 cup chopped onion
1/2 cup chopped celery
1/4 cup chopped carrot
2 garlic cloves, minced
4 cups peeled, seeded, diced fresh tomatoes
    or 2 (16-oz.) cans tomatoes

1 teaspoon dried oregano
1/4 teaspoon dried thyme
1/4 teaspoon dried basil
1 teaspoon salt
1/8 teaspoon black pepper
1 teaspoon sugar

In a large saucepan, heat oil and butter. Sauté onion, celery, carrot and garlic in oil and butter until onion is golden. Add tomatoes, oregano, thyme, basil, salt, pepper and sugar. Bring to a boil. Cover. Simmer 1 hour. Uncover and simmer 1 hour longer. Sauce may be stored in refrigerator 1 week or sauce may be frozen. Makes about 4 cups.

Serving Suggestions: Spoon sauce over hot cooked wide noodles made from Whole-Wheat Pasta, page 15, or Plain Pasta, page 14.

To peel a tomato: Let the tomato stand in boiling water about 20 seconds. Cut out the stem and peel off the skin starting from the stem end. To remove the seeds and juice, cut the tomato in half crosswise and gently squeeze each half.

Desserts

Pasta is not something usually associated with sugar and spices. However, in working with pasta I discovered an array of exciting new desserts!

Orzo, the barley-like pasta is a good substitute for rice in puddings. Try it in Creamy Orzo Pudding. *Risino*, or *rice macaroni*, is another good rice substitute. I used it in Cocoa Pudding. Then I combined risino with coconut and came up with a tasty No-Crust Coconut Pie!

Sweet Dessert Manicotti, page 20, is a pasta-like thin pancake or crepe. Try Rum-Buttered Bananas Manicotti, Apricot Strata, Manicotti With Butterscotch Sauce and Berry-Yogurt Manicotti. To save time, cook the manicotti the day before and refrigerate it.

Noodle puddings are always good for entertaining because they serve many and can be made in advance. Pineapple Noodle Pudding can be served plain or with sour cream.

Chocolate Dessert Pasta, page 20, unlike the other pastas, calls for toasting the flour in the oven before it is mixed into a dough. The pasta does not have to be boiled but can be shaped and then baked. The dough used for Petite Chocolate Sandwiches is versatile enough to make dessert garnishes. Roll out the leftover dough and cut fancy shapes such as half-moons or stars. Bake them 3 minutes in a preheated 350°F (175°C) oven. Then cool them before storing in an airtight container. These pretty pasta wafers make an intriguing garnish for sundaes or toppings.

Menu
For That Special Evening
Chicken Consommé
Orange-Glazed Cornish Game Hens
Orange Pasta Noodles, page 14
Green Beans Almondine
Waldorf Salad
Butterflake Dinner Crescents
Rum-Buttered Bananas Manicotti, page 157
Coffee

Berry-Yogurt Manicotti

Try fresh fruit or berries in season for an extra special treat.

2 cups sliced fresh strawberries
1/2 cup sugar
1 carton plain yogurt (1 cup)

8 Sweet Dessert Manicotti, page 20
8 whole strawberries for garnish

Sprinkle sliced strawberries with sugar. Let stand 30 minutes. Mix 1/2 cup yogurt and strawberry-sugar mixture. Spread about 4 tablespoons yogurt-strawberry mixture down center of each manicotti. Fold sides over mixture. Spoon 1 tablespoon remaining yogurt over each filled manicotti. Place 1 whole strawberry on each dollop of yogurt. Serve immediately. Makes 4 to 8 servings.

Chocolate-Covered Cherries

Reminiscent of cherry cordials.

Chocolate Dessert Pasta dough, page 20   2 tablespoons butter, melted
30 whole red or green candied cherries

Preheat oven to 350°F (175°C). Lightly butter a baking sheet; set aside. Roll about 1 tablespoon Chocolate Dessert Pasta dough around each whole candied cherry. Cover entire cherry to make a 1-inch ball. Brush each ball with melted butter. Place on prepared baking sheet. Bake in preheated oven, 3 minutes. Place on a wire rack to cool. Makes about 30 Chocolate Covered Cherries.

Chocolate Cornucopias

Serve soon after filling so the cornucopias don't become soggy.

Chocolate Dessert Pasta dough, page 20   Candied cherry pieces for garnish
2 tablespoons butter, melted   Walnut halves for garnish
Whipped cream

Preheat oven to 350°F (175°C). Divide Chocolate Dessert Pasta dough into 4 parts. Place in plastic bag and let rest 10 minutes. Roll out dough by hand or with a pasta machine 1/8 inch thick. With a pastry wheel, cut dough into 2-inch squares. Continue until all the dough is rolled and cut. Bring 2 opposite corners of each square up and overlap, leaving a wide opening at 1 end and little or no opening at the other end. Crumple small pieces of aluminum foil and place in the wide opening of each cornucopia to hold its shape. Lightly brush tops and sides with melted butter. Place on an un-greased cookie sheet. Bake in preheated oven, 3 minutes. Do not overbake. Carefully place on wire rack to cool. Remove foil. To serve, fill cooled cornucopias with whipped cream. Garnish with a candied cherry piece or walnut halves. Serve immediately. Makes 20 to 25 cornucopias.

Petite Chocolate Sandwiches

You don't really need a scalloped cookie cutter to make these. A plain one will do.

Chocolate Dessert Pasta dough, page 20   Sifted powdered sugar for topping
1 pt. vanilla, mint or peppermint ice cream

Preheat oven to 350°F (175°C). Divide Chocolate Dessert Pasta dough into 4 equal parts. Place dough in a plastic bag. Let rest 10 minutes. Roll out dough by hand or with a pasta machine 1/16 inch thick. Cut dough with a 2-inch scalloped cookie cutter. Place cut dough on cookie sheet. Continue cutting until all dough is used. Bake in preheated oven 3 minutes. Remove baked wafers from cookie sheet. Cool completely on a wire rack. Working quickly, cut ice cream into 1/2-inch slices. Then cut slices with the cookie cutter. Place an ice cream cut-out on a chocolate wafer. Place a second chocolate wafer on top of the ice cream. Continue until all wafers are used. Freeze 1 hour before serving. Makes 20 to 30 sandwiches.

From top right: Chocolate Covered Cherries, Petite Chocolate Sandwiches and Chocolate Cornucopias

No-Crust Coconut Pie

Like magic, tiny rice-like pasta and coconut form the crust.

3 cups milk
1/2 cup risino
4 eggs
1/2 cup sugar
1/4 teaspoon baking powder

1/4 cup butter, melted
1 cup angel flake coconut
1 teaspoon vanilla extract
Cinnamon for topping

Preheat oven to 350°F (175°C). Butter a 10-inch pie plate. In a 2-quart saucepan, bring 2 cups milk and risino to a boil over medium heat, stirring constantly. Reduce heat and continue stirring 15 minutes. In a large bowl, using a fork or whisk, lightly beat eggs. Beat in remaining 1 cup milk, sugar, baking powder, melted butter, coconut, vanilla and cooked milk mixture. Pour into prepared pie plate. Bake in preheated oven until golden brown, 45 to 50 minutes. Remove from oven; cool on wire rack. Dust with cinnamon while warm. Makes 6 to 8 servings.

Pasta Puffs

Puffs may be sprinkled with powdered sugar, as pictured, instead of the syrup and nut mixture.

Egg Noodle Pasta dough, page 14
Oil for deep-frying
1/2 cup finely chopped walnuts

1/8 teaspoon cinnamon
Honey Syrup, see below

Honey Syrup:
1 cup honey
1/3 cup hot water

1 teaspoon lemon juice

Divide Egg Noodle Pasta dough into 6 balls. If using a pasta machine, roll immediately. If rolling by hand, place dough in a plastic bag and let rest 1 hour before rolling out on a lightly floured board. Roll out dough almost paper-thin. Cut into 5" x 4" rectangles. Layer rectangles between sheets of waxed paper until all 6 balls of dough are rolled and cut. In an electric skillet or in a wide pot, pre-heat oil to 375°F (190°C). At this temperature, a 1-inch cube of bread will turn golden brown in 40 seconds. Carefully place 1 pasta rectangle at a time into the hot oil. Fry until lightly browned, about 5 seconds. Using 2 forks, immediately turn over and fold in half. Work quickly; puffs become crisp rapidly and will not fold easily. Drain on paper towels. Mix walnuts and cinnamon. Prepare Honey Syrup; set aside. Drizzle Honey Syrup over puffs. Sprinkle puffs with the nut mixture. Makes 30 to 40 puffs.

Honey Syrup:
In a small bowl, mix 1 cup honey, 1/3 cup hot water and 1 teaspoon lemon juice.

How To Make
Pasta Puffs

1/Carefully place paper-thin pasta rectangles 1 at a time into hot oil.

2/When pasta begins to bubble and puff, use 2 forks to gently fold rectangles in half. Turn and fry until crisp and lightly browned.

3/Drain puffs on paper towels. Sprinkle with powdered sugar or top with Honey Syrup and chopped nuts.

Apple Noodle Pudding

Honey and brown sugar sweeten this colorful dessert.

2 cups water
1/2 teaspoon salt
1 teaspoon vegetable oil
3/4 cup noodle squares (4 oz.)
1-1/2 tablespoons cornstarch
3/4 cup orange juice

2 tablespoons butter
2 tablespoons honey
1/4 cup firmly packed brown sugar
1 teaspoon lemon juice
2 medium apples, cored, diced
Sprigs of mint for garnish

Bring water to a rapid boil in a heavy 2-quart saucepan. Add salt and oil. Gradually add noodle squares, being sure water continues to boil. Cook noodle squares uncovered until tender but firm, stirring occasionally. Drain; set aside. In a small saucepan, blend cornstarch and orange juice. Cook over medium heat until thickened, stirring constantly. Remove from heat. Add butter, honey, brown sugar and lemon juice. Stir until butter is melted. Stir in apples. Heat through. Spoon over cooked noodle squares; mix well. Divide into 4 serving dishes. Chill before serving. Garnish with sprigs of mint. Makes 4 servings.

Pineapple Noodle Pudding

Leave off the sour cream and it's a delightful side dish for ham.

6 cups water
1/2 Pineapple Pasta dough, page 14,
   cut in noodles, uncooked, or
   4 cups medium noodles (8 oz.)
1/2 cup butter or margarine
5 eggs

2 cups dairy sour cream
1 cup sugar
1/2 teaspoon grated orange peel
1/4 teaspoon cinnamon
2 (8-oz.) cans crushed pineapple, drained
Dairy sour cream for topping

Bring water to a rapid boil in a heavy 3-quart saucepan. Gradually add noodles, being sure water continues to boil. Cook noodles uncovered until tender but firm, stirring occasionally. Drain. Preheat oven to 350°F (175°C). Place butter in a 13" x 9" baking dish and melt in the oven. In a large bowl beat eggs. Stir in 2 cups sour cream, sugar, orange peel and cinnamon. Add pineapple and cooked noodles. Spread melted butter over bottom of dish. Pour excess butter into egg mixture; stir. Pour egg mixture into prepared baking dish. Bake in preheated oven until golden, 45 minutes. Serve warm topped with sour cream. Pudding may be made ahead and served cold or may be warmed in a 350°F (175°C) oven 20 minutes. Makes 18 servings.

Orange Pasta and Pineapple Pasta are sweet doughs and should be cooked in unsalted water.

Easy Noodle Pudding

Raisin-Rum Sauce adds the finishing touch.

5 cups water
1 teaspoon salt
1 teaspoon oil
3 cups medium noodles, uncooked
3 eggs

2 cups half-and-half
1 cup sugar
1/2 teaspoon cinnamon
Rum Sauce, see below
Whipped cream for garnish

Raisin-Rum Sauce:

1-1/2 cups water
1/4 cup white raisins
1/4 cup currants
1/4 cup sugar
2 tablespoons butter

1-1/2 tablespoons cornstarch
2 tablespoons cold water
1/4 cup coarsely chopped walnuts
2 tablespoons rum

Butter an 8-inch square baking dish; set aside. Preheat oven to 300°F (150°C). Bring water to a rapid boil in a heavy 3-quart saucepan. Add salt and oil. Gradually add noodles, being sure water continues to boil. Cook noodles uncovered until tender but firm, stirring occasionally. Drain. While noodles cook, beat eggs in a medium bowl. Stir in half-and-half, sugar and cinnamon. Pour over cooked noodles. Gently toss to coat. Spoon into prepared baking dish. Bake in preheated oven until a knife inserted off center comes out clean; about 1 hour. Prepare Raisin-Rum Sauce. Keep warm. Remove pudding from oven. Cut into eight 4" x 2" pieces. Serve hot or cold with warm Rum-Raisin Sauce. Garnish with whipped cream. Makes 8 servings.

Raisin-Rum Sauce:

In a small saucepan, bring 1-1/2 cups water to a boil. Remove from heat. Add raisins and currants. Let stand 10 minutes. Stir in sugar and butter. Cook over medium heat until mixture comes to a boil. Dissolve cornstarch in 2 tablespoons water. Stir into boiling water mixture. Continue cooking and stirring until thickened. Remove from heat; stir in walnuts and rum. Makes 2 cups.

Cocoa Pudding

Freeze dollops of whipped cream on a greased cookie sheet for ready homemade topping.

2 cups milk
1/2 cup risino
1/4 cup sugar
1/2 cup unsweetened cocoa powder

Salt to taste
1 teaspoon vanilla extract
Whipped cream for garnish

In a 2-quart saucepan, bring milk and risino to a boil over medium heat, stirring constantly. Reduce heat to low. Cook and stir about 15 minutes. Stir in sugar, cocoa powder and salt. Cook 2 minutes longer. Remove from heat and add vanilla. Pour into six 1/2-cup serving bowls or dessert dishes. Serve warm, garnished with whipped cream. Makes 6 servings.

Apricot Strata

To save time and energy, use a pressure can of whipped cream.

16 Sweet Dessert Manicotti, page 20
3/4 cup apricot-pineapple preserves
1/3 cup chopped walnuts

8 scoops vanilla ice cream
Whipped cream for garnish
4 maraschino cherries, cut in half, for garnish

Spread each Sweet Dessert Manicotti with 1 teaspoon preserves. On a large platter or serving tray, place 8 manicotti, preserve-side up. Sprinkle each with 1 teaspoon chopped walnuts. Place remaining 8 manicotti over nuts, preserve-side up. Top each with 1 scoop of ice cream. Pipe whipped cream around the scoops of ice cream. Sprinkle each with an additional 1 teaspoon chopped walnuts. Garnish with half a maraschino cherry. Makes 8 servings.

Bavarian Strudel

Cut the remaining dough into noodles.

1/3 Egg Noodle Pasta dough, page 14
Applie Filling, see below
1 tablespoon butter, melted

2 cups hot milk
Powdered sugar for garnish

Apple Filling:
3 cups, finely sliced, peeled apples
  (3 to 4 baking apples)
1/2 cup sugar
1/2 cup finely chopped walnuts

1/3 cup coarse dry breadcrumbs
1/4 cup golden raisins
1/2 teaspoon cinnamon
Nutmeg to taste

Preheat oven to 400°F (205°C). Butter a 13" x 9" baking dish. **If using a pasta machine,** divide dough into 3 balls and roll out immediately. Roll each ball of dough into 3 paper thin strips, 18" x 6". Overlap the strips lengthwise to make an 18-inch square. **If rolling out by hand,** place dough in a plastic bag and let rest 30 minutes, then on a lightly floured board, roll out dough to an 18-inch square. Spread dough with Apple Filling, leaving a 1/2-inch strip uncovered on one edge. Roll up jelly-roll fashion toward uncovered edge. Pinch with fingers along edge to seal. Place in prepared baking dish seam-side down, curving slightly to fit in dish. Brush top with melted butter. Pour hot milk over strudel. Bake until golden in preheated oven, 20 minutes. Cut into six 3-inch sections. Place each section of strudel into a dessert dish. Spoon hot milk over the strudel. Sprinkle with powdered sugar. Makes 6 servings.

Apple Filling:
Combine all ingredients in a large bowl.

Variation

Substitute 1 (1-lb.-5-oz.) can cherry pie filling for apples. Mix 1/2 cup chopped nuts and 1/4 cup raisins with pie filling.

Creamy Orzo Pudding

Curl thin strips of lemon peel around your finger for a different and pretty garnish.

3 cups milk
3/4 cup orzo
1/3 cup sugar
1/4 teaspoon nutmeg
Salt to taste

1 teaspoon grated lemon peel
2 egg yolks
1 teaspoon vanilla extract
Dash nutmeg or mace for garnish

In a 2-quart saucepan, bring milk and orzo to a boil, stirring constantly. Reduce heat to low. Cook 30 to 35 minutes, stirring occasionally. Blend in sugar, nutmeg, salt and lemon peel. Beat egg yolks in a small bowl. Gradually stir 1/2 cup hot milk mixture into egg yolks. Slowly stir egg mixture and vanilla into pudding. Pour into six 1/2-cup serving bowls or dessert dishes. Garnish with nutmeg or mace. Serve warm or cover with plastic wrap and refrigerate before serving. Makes 6 servings.

Cherry Turnovers

Lightly flour the top of a large drinking glass and use it to cut circles from the dough.

2 eggs, slightly beaten
1/2 cup water
3 tablespoons vegetable oil
3 tablespoons sugar
1/4 teaspoon salt

3 cups all-purpose flour
1 (1-lb. 5-oz.) can cherry pie filling
Oil for deep-frying
Powdered sugar for garnish, if desired

In a large bowl, combine eggs, water, oil, sugar and salt. Stir in flour 1 cup at a time, to make a stiff dough. Let dough rest 5 minutes. Knead until smooth, 8 to 10 minutes. Divide dough into 3 equal balls. Place balls in a plastic bag; let rest 1 hour. On a lightly floured board, roll each ball of dough 1/8 inch thick. Use a biscuit cutter to cut 3-inch circles. With your hands, stretch each circle slightly. Drain sauce from cherries; reserve sauce. Place 2 whole drained cherries on half of each circle. Do not use any of the cherry sauce. Fold dough over to make a half circle. Seal edges by pressing with the tines of a fork. Turnovers may be made several hours ahead and refrigerated before frying. Preheat oil in a deep pot to 375°F (190°C). At this temperature, a 1-inch cube of bread will turn golden brown in 40 seconds. Deep-fry turnovers a few at a time until golden, 2 minutes. Drain on paper towels. Heat reserved cherry sauce in a small saucepan. Spoon over fried turnovers, or serve dry with a sprinkling of powdered sugar. Serve immediately. Makes 3 to 4 dozen.

Lemon Squares

Prepare this lemon-rich dessert the day before you plan to serve it.

4 cups water
1/2 teaspoon salt
1/2 Lemon Pasta dough, page 14,
   cut in noodles, uncooked, or
   2 cups medium noodles (4 oz.)
1/3 cup half-and-half
1/2 cup flaked coconut
1/2 cup chopped walnuts

1 egg, slightly beaten
1 tablespoon granulated sugar
1/4 teaspoon cinnamon
4 oz. cream cheese, softened
1/2 cup dairy sour cream
2 tablespoons powdered sugar
1 (1-lb.-6-oz.) can lemon pie filling

Bring water to a rapid boil in a heavy 2-quart saucepan. Add salt. Gradually add noodles, being sure water continues to boil. Cook noodles uncovered until tender but firm, stirring occasionally. Drain. Preheat oven to 350°F (175°C). Butter a 9-inch square glass baking dish; set aside. In a medium bowl, toss together cooked noodles, half-and-half, coconut, walnuts, egg, granulated sugar and cinnamon. Spoon into prepared baking dish. Bake in preheated oven 20 minutes. Cool 10 minutes: Refrigerate 20 minutes. In a small bowl, stir softened cream cheese. Blend in sour cream and powdered sugar. Spread over cooled noodle base. Refrigerate 30 minutes longer. Spread lemon pie filling over top of cheese mixture. Refrigerate 30 minutes before serving. Makes 9 servings.

Jewish Kugel

You'll also enjoy this as a side dish, without the sour cream and preserves.

1 tablespoon lemon juice
1 cup shredded tart apples, drained
6 cups water
1 teaspoon salt
2 teaspoons vegetable oil
4 cups medium noodles (8 oz.) or
   1/2 Plain Pasta dough, page 14,
   cut in noodles, uncooked

1/2 cup butter or margarine
3 eggs
2 cups dairy sour cream
1/2 cup light raisins
1/3 cup sugar
1/2 teaspoon cinnamon
Dairy sour cream for garnish
Cherry or strawberry preserves for garnish

Mix lemon juice with shredded apples, set aside. Bring water to a rapid boil in a heavy 3-quart saucepan. Add salt and oil. Gradually add noodles, being sure water continues to boil. Cook noodles uncovered until tender but firm, stirring occasionally. Drain. Preheat oven to 350°F (175°C). Place butter in an 11" x 7" baking dish and melt in the oven. In a large bowl beat eggs. Stir in 2 cups sour cream, shredded apples, raisins, sugar and cinnamon. Add cooked noodles. Spread melted butter over bottom of dish. Pour excess butter into egg mixture; stir. Spoon into prepared baking dish. Bake in preheated oven until golden, 45 minutes. Serve warm topped with sour cream or preserves. Pudding may be made ahead and served cold, or warmed in a 350°F (175°C) oven 20 minutes. Makes 8 servings.

Manicotti With Butterscotch Sauce

Make these up ahead and freeze them for a special dessert on a busy day.

1 (6-oz.) pkg. butterscotch chips (1 cup)
1/2 cup sweetened condensed milk
1 tablespoon milk or half-and-half
6 scoops vanilla ice cream, softened

6 Sweet Dessert Manicotti, page 20
Whipped cream for garnish
Toasted slivered almond for garnish

In a double boiler or a small pan inside a larger pan, melt butterscotch chips over low heat, stirring occasionally. Stir in sweetened condensed milk and milk or half-and-half. Heat and stir milk mixture; do not boil. Set aside to cool. Spread 1 scoop of ice cream over each Dessert Manicotti. Roll up jelly-roll fashion. Place seam-side down on a small platter. Freeze until set, 30 minutes. Serve with butter-scotch sauce. Garnish with whipped cream and toasted slivered almonds. Makes 6 rolls.

Crispy Treats

Delicious pastry-like bows are sprinkled with powdered sugar.

1 egg
2 cups milk
1/4 cup firmly packed brown sugar
1/8 teaspoon salt

6 cups flour
Oil for deep-frying
Granulated sugar or sifted powdered sugar
   for topping

Beat egg in a large bowl. Add milk, brown sugar and salt. Gradually stir in flour, 2 cups at a time. When dough forms a ball, knead on a lightly floured board until smooth and elastic, 4 minutes. Let dough rest 10 minutes. Divide into 6 equal balls. Roll out each ball by hand or with a pasta machine 1/16 inch thick. Cut into 4" x 2-1/2" rectangles. Each ball makes 20 to 25. Pinch center of each rectangle to form a bow. Preheat oil for deep-frying in a deep heavy pot. Attach deep-fry ther-mometer to side of pan; heat oil to 375°F (190°C). At this temperature, a 1-inch cube of bread will turn brown in 40 seconds. Using a slotted spoon, lower bows into the hot oil. Cook until golden brown, 2 to 3 seconds on each side. Turn gently, using 2 forks. Drain on paper towels. While warm, sprinkle with granulated sugar or sifted powdered sugar. Makes 120 to 150 bows.

Variation

For a different shape, dough may be cut into 3-inch or 6-inch squares and cut into triangles.

Rum-Buttered Bananas Manicotti

The sauce may be prepared ahead, but filled manicotti should be eaten immediately.

1 tablespoon cornstarch	1 to 2 tablespoons rum
3/4 cup milk	6 scoops vanilla ice cream, softened
1 cup firmly packed light brown sugar	6 Sweet Dessert Manicotti, page 20
1/4 cup light corn syrup	3 small bananas
2 tablespoons butter	Whipped cream for topping

In a small saucepan, stir cornstarch into milk. Add brown sugar and corn syrup. Stir constantly over medium heat until thickened. Remove from heat. Stir in butter and rum; set aside. Spread 1 scoop ice cream on one side of each Sweet Dessert Manicotti. Peel and slice bananas in half lengthwise. Place half a banana over ice cream. Fold manicotti in half to cover banana and ice cream. Pour warm sauce over filled manicotti. Top with whipped cream. Serve immediately. Makes 6 servings.

How To Make
Rum-Buttered Bananas Manicotti

1/Spread softened ice cream on one side of manicotti. Place 1/2 peeled banana over ice cream. Fold edge over.

2/Before serving, pour rum-butter sauce over ice cream and banana filled manicotti.

Index